The WORLD at WAR

igloobooks

igloobooks

Published in 2013
by Igloo Books Ltd
Cottage Farm
Sywell
NN6 0BJ
www.igloobooks.com

SHE001 0913
2 4 6 8 10 9 7 5 3 1
ISBN 978-1-78197-893-1

Printed and manufactured in China

The WORLD at WAR

Contents

World War Two

Introduction

I n many respects, the modern world has become defined by the two world wars. A century after the beginning of World War I, we now have the benefit of a hundred years hindsight to see just how things have been changed so much by worldwide conflict.

Perhaps the most obvious changes were technological. The arms race prompted by the desire to win the war, on both sides, meant that many areas of technology advanced dramatically during World War I (1914-18) and World War II (1939-45). The interwar period (1918-39) and the post-war period (1945-) have both seen marked technological progress for similar reasons. Even in the absence of conflict, the technological world war has continued unabated.

The areas of technological progress included transport (on land, through water and in air), communication (radio), computing (code breaking), detection (sonar, radar and reconnaissance), ordnance (weapons and ammunition), medicine (antibiotics), materials (composites), energy (nuclear), propulsion (jets and rockets).

Just about every area of science, technology, engineering and manufacture was pushed forward by necessity. If it meant having an edge over the enemy, then it was usually worth the investment of time, effort, expertise and money

From a military point of view, advances in technology also resulted in a requirement for different strategic thinking. Battles on land and at sea were no longer a matter of meeting up and slogging it out until one side emerged the victor. It became necessary to work out ways of keeping the frontline dynamic and mobile, to avoid the stalemate of entrenchment. It also became necessary to figure out ways of invading coastlines

from the sea and how best to utilize or defend against new phenomena, such as aircraft, tanks and submarines. The machines of war would come to dominate the battlefield as a defining characteristic of modern warfare.

There have also been great societal shifts, for the better, in terms of class structure and gender role. The deaths of so many men meant that traditional class structures were eroded and more women stepped into the shoes of traditionally male professions. There was also a fundamental change in the way humanity regarded itself, partly due to bewilderment at the destruction it had wrought upon itself as a single species. Also, there was utter shock at mans inhumanity to man, which betrayed an underlying animalistic nature that people had preferred to think was a trait lost in our prehistory.

On the international level, the world wars caused considerable changes to the political map. Ironically, the wars themselves had largely been about ambitions of territorial conquest, which were duly prevented, yet the movements of borders were considerable in the wake of conflict as the new world order was established. Empires fragmented, while new empires were created.

At the root of all of the horrific and wasteful bloodshed were concepts of difference between populations. The human ability to adopt varying beliefs, ideologies, philosophies, politics, ethics and morals is a defining characteristic of our species. To be so, it must have served an advantageous purpose in our distant evolutionary past, but the world wars demonstrated quite clearly that it now had the potential to make humanity destroy itself. Perhaps this is the most valuable lesson to have come from two global conflicts-that the human condition is flawed, because our future would be better served if we evolved psychological alignment and harmony.

British troops go forward in 'No Man's Land', Battle of the Somme, 1916

WORLD WAR ONE

British troops moving up to the trenches, 2.5 miles East of Ypres

Franz Ferdinand (1863 - 1914),
Archduke of Austria, heir-apparent
to the emperor Franz Joseph

How the Trigger was Pulled

In the years prior to World War I, the political map of Europe was quite different from the present era. Some of the countries we know today were still evolving in terms of their territorial boundaries and ethnic tensions were running high in central and eastern regions.

At the heart of this area was the Austro-Hungarian Empire, which comprised lands that are now recognized as, all or part of, no fewer than fourteen countries. Naturally, the ethnic minority populations disliked having their lands held by the Empire and they disliked the regime of oppression placed on their peoples, from the Austrians and the Hungarians.

A Bosnian Serb, named Gavrilo Princip, had enough of living under the empirical thumb. He joined a nationalist paramilitary movement named the Black Hand, whose ambition it was to fight for Serbian independence.

In June 1914, Princip and his comrades learnt that the heir to the Austro-Hungarian throne, Archduke Franz Ferdinand, would be making an official visit to Sarajevo, so they hatched a plot to assassinate him in the name of their cause. On the 28th the Black Hand prepared to carry out their plan, but things went wrong and the Archduke escaped unharmed. However, following the visit his driver took a backstreet to avoid the possibility of a further attempt on the Archduke's life.

It just so happened that the dejected Princip was walking along that very same backstreet. He immediately seized his opportunity and shot both the Archduke and his wife at close range. The job was done, but Princip could not imagine the chain of events he had started by succeeding in assassinating the Archduke.

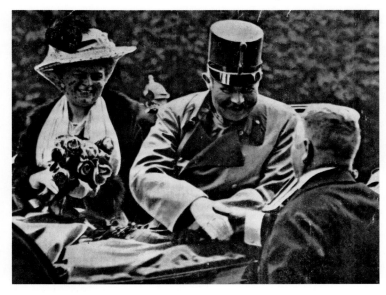

The Archduke and his wife, Sophie shortly before their assassination in Sarajevo

The Austro-Hungarians wanted to take their revenge on the Serbian kingdom, amassed troops on the border and declared war. This prompted much political manoeuvring among the powers of Europe, according to historical allegiances. Just a month after the assassination, and the entire sub-continent was poised for war as all parties took their sides.

As for Princip, well he languished in prison for the next few years, where he eventually died from tuberculosis some months before World War I came to a close. His dream of an independent Serbia would not become a reality until the end of the 20th century and the region remains in a state of political tension due to ethnic divisions and political schisms. The Austro-Hungarian Empire was officially dissolved on the 31st October, 1918, eleven days before the official ceasefire of The Great War.

Serbian student Gavrilo Princip, who assassinated Franz Ferdinand

Taking Sides

In the month following the Assassination of the Archduke Franz Ferdinand, the European nations took sides in preparation for all-out war, on a scale never seen before. The British Empire allied with the French and Russian Empires, to form the Triple Entente. The Austro-Hungarian Empire joined with the German Empire to form the Central Powers. Italy had initially agreed to join the Central Powers, but switched sides following the London Pact of 1915. The Italians had ambitions of building an empire, so the Entente promised them new territories as a reward for their allegiance.

A number of other European nations remained neutral, as they either had no vested interest in going to war, or they had no bellicose inclinations. They included the countries of the Iberian Peninsula, Scandinavia and South-eastern Europe. Serbia and Montenegro allied with the Russian Empire as part of the Entente. Switzerland remained neutral despite its being smack bang in the middle of the war zone.

Front page of French newspaper Le Petit Journal: Death to the Monster – France, England, Serbia, Russia and Belgium have declared war to Germany and Austria

King Carol I of Romania from 1881. At the beginning of World War I he declared Romania neutral

As the key participants of the Entente and the Central Powers were empires, this meant that they each possessed territories and populations in other parts of the world. Although most of the fighting would take place in Europe, those involved were from a truly international collection of colonies, from all five continents. This is why it became known as the First World War, as opposed to The European War. Many described it as The Great War, until World War II superseded it in terms of scale.

Unfortunately, for the Central Powers, their combined empires were far smaller than those of the Entente, which immediately gave them a disadvantage, both in terms of material resources and available personnel. Despite the clear likelihood that they would ultimately lose the war, they chose to commence hostilities on the 28th July 1914. It seems that a combination of Teutonic pride and empirical ambition gave the enemy, who would widely become known collectively as the Hun or the Bosche, an over-inflated idea of their destiny, leaving them hell-bent on expanding their realm on the map of Europe and on the map of the World as a consequence of conquest.

The famous World War I recruiting poster featuring Lord Kitchener

A recruitment drive during the First World War at Trafalgar Square, London

Army recruits taking the oath at offices in White City, 1914

Blind Enthusiasm

A good deal of discussion has been conducted over the fact that most British soldiers volunteered to go to war in the initial stages. That is to say, conscription was not really required, because so many British men were enthusiastic about the idea of becoming soldiers and serving their country. So enthusiastic, in fact, that those considered too young to fight would often pretend to be older, and those considered too old would often pretend to be younger.

This blind enthusiasm seems to have resulted from a combination of factors in British society at that time in history. For one thing, very few people had first-hand experience of warfare in the Edwardian period, so most had little idea of the true horrors awaiting them. In addition, Britain was a rather staid and predictable environment, so the idea of adventure abroad was a very inviting prospect. There was also a strong sense of belonging to the great empire, so that men wanted to play their part in the war for fear of being seen of in a negative light by society.

British Army recruitment poster, 1917

It is also important to remember that there was a very clear class structure in Britain as a hangover from the Victorian era. The working class had laborious lives of subservience, repetition and drudgery. The middle class had tedious lives of pen pushing and managerial duties. The upper class had idle lives of hunting and sporting in imitation of true challenge. Not surprisingly, men from all three classes were excited by the prospect of donning uniforms and going overseas to give the enemy their dues.

In their minds it amounted to an adventure holiday, firing guns and enjoying a macho environment for a few months, before returning home with something to talk about for the rest of their lives. Very few seem to have had any real notion that there would be no more of their lives to enjoy. This was compounded by the propaganda used to invite them to war in the first place and the notion that warfare was no longer a matter of hand-to-hand combat, but rather something conducted over a civilized distance between friend and foe.

After eighteen months of fighting, the reality of modern warfare had become clear. So many men had been slaughtered on the killing fields that conscription was introduced for all men between the ages of 18 and 41 with the Military Service Act 1916. By 1918, the upper-age parameter had been raised to 51 years in order to compensate for the woeful losses on the Western Front. A young army had been all but replaced by a middle aged army.

Infantrymen sitting in a trench reading and smoking during the early days of trench warfare

British soldiers in the trenches during World War I, 1914

Entrenchment

When World War I broke out, on 28th July 1914, the Central Powers launched a campaign to reach the English Channel by advancing into France. This became known as the Race to the Sea and followed a number of opening battles in the war. These included the Battle of the Marne and the Battle of the Aisne. The original intention of the German Imperial Army had been to take Paris, but this ambition had been thwarted by the Allies, so the Germans tried a new tactic.

As the Germans tried to fight their way to the coast, the French and British forces resisted. Many subsequent attacks and counter-attacks eventually led to a stalemate situation in the region of Artois and Flanders. The result was a more-or-less static frontline between the opposing forces. So it was, that the Western Front became a north-south line, stretching from Nieuport in Belgium down towards Paris in France.

Due to the stasis, both sides were forced to settle into a prolonged trench war. Once in a while, offensives and counter-offensives would move the frontline westward and eastward, but never any considerable distance. This meant that the same swathe of fighting terrain was occupied for about four years. As a consequence, the landscape became a featureless expanse of mud as hundreds of thousands of shells destroyed the trees and plowed the soil with their explosions. Buildings and roads suffered the same treatment, so that the battlegrounds became panoramas in shades of brown, with little to distinguish one place from another, save the odd ruin, tree stump, hill or stream.

German invasion of France: gray hordes of infantrymen stream forward relentlessly through the peaceful sunlit fields of France

With every feature razed to the ground, it also meant nowhere to hide. The only option, for both sides, was to live a subterranean existence in trenches, tunnels and dugouts. Conditions were unpleasant to say the least. Not only did soldiers have to contend with unsanitary and damp conditions, but the land around them was strewn with the decomposing fragments of corpses. The winters brought constant muddy wetness and cold, while the summers brought the stench of putrefaction.

Then there were the animal pests to deal with: maggots and flies, hair and body lice, rats and mice. As eradication was impossible, the soldiers could only do their best to avoid infestations by keeping their environment relatively clean. Another serious problem was 'trench foot'. The footwear of soldiers allowed their feet to get damp and cold for prolonged periods of time. This resulted in swelling and secondary infections, which would lead to painful skin peeling and even loss of toes, rendering combatants unable to fight effectively.

British tommies relaxing and having wounds treated in an underground forward dressing station by the Menin Road in France

The Eastern Front

As the main Allied campaign was at the Western Front during World War I, it is often forgotten that there was also an Eastern Front. This is where the Russians, and their allies, took on the Austro-Hungarian army. Thus, the Central Powers had to fight on two flanks, in an effort to increase their empire both eastward and westward. Needless to say, it meant having to spread their resources with inevitable consequences in the long run.

At that time, Russia was in a state of political unrest and its infrastructure was not geared up to the material demands of war on this unprecedented scale. What it did have, however, was a vast population, so it was able to keep replenishing its battalions with new personnel. Nevertheless, the Russian people soon grew disillusioned by the sheer war effort and the enormously high casualty rate. To all intents and purposes, it felt as if the Russian monarchy was treating the war as if it were a giant game of chess, with human cost all part of the game.

Ultimately, this lack of concern for the common people led to revolution in February 1917. Tsar Nicholas was forced to abdicate and the Communist Bolsheviks took power, under the leadership of Vladimir Lenin. Having a new cause to fight for gave the Russian army a morale boost, putting the enemy forces on the back foot. Then the Communists attempted to cease hostilities with the Central Powers, but this resulted in a large-scale offensive from the enemy, sensing weakness in the Russian resolve, due to their own civil war.

Action in a British first line trench
in the Balkans, Eastern Front

Adorned with flowers, a soldier of the
Austro-Hungarian army prepares to
leave for the Eastern Front

The Eastern Front finally fell peaceful in March 1918, with the Treaty of Brest-Litovsk. This enabled the Central Powers to divert their spare forces to the Western Front in the hope of finally winning the war. However, it was too late, as the US had declared war on Germany and begun sending troops to France and Belgium, thereby countering the additional manpower.

Unlike the Western Front, the Eastern Front was far more mobile, in both directions, which meant that trench warfare did not typify the theatre of war in that region. This had a good deal to do with the terrain, which was not generally flat and deeply soiled, but far more hilly and mountainous instead. As a result, offensives and counter-offensives moved the frontline considerable distances, as one force advanced and the other retreated.

German soldiers operating a machine gun from a trench on Russia's Eastern Front

American soldiers practising with camouflaged artillery after their arrival in France in 1917

Camouflage

It may be hard to believe, but in the initial stages of World War I, the French wore their traditional blue coats and red trousers on the battlefield. Needless to say, they stood out like sore thumbs against the greens and browns of the countryside and were easily targeted by the German riflemen, artillerymen and particularly the machine gunners. Before too long, the high command admitted that it might be better to give their troops a fighting chance, so they introduced a more neutral coloured uniform in grayish-blue, which was still pretty visible but a marked improvement.

The British had already learnt the value of mimicking the colours of battle terrain in the late 19th century, so they entered the war wearing uniforms in khaki, which is a drab, olive-green colour. Although khaki was a better colour than grayish-blue, both uniforms were still visible to one extent or another, because the background often comprised many hues and tones. Textile technologies were not able to produce the complex patterns needed for more successful camouflage, but this realization led to rapid camouflage developments in other areas on the field of battle.

Machines of war, such as artillery guns, tanks and troop carriers were soon being painted in contrasting shades and colours, to obscure their outlines and make it more difficult for the enemy to interpret what they were seeing. These developments were accelerated by the introduction of aircraft into the theatre of war. As aircraft were able to view enemy activities from a vantage point, it became increasingly important to hide equipment and personnel. This resulted in the use of camouflaged canvas and netting for the purpose of concealment from above.

As the terrain at the Western Front was typically flat and featureless, it was very obvious if anyone so much as raised their head above the parapet, making reconnaissance rather dangerous. This led to the invention of artificial trees in the hope of gaining an elevated view without being shot. Steel-frame pylons would be hastily erected at night and then camouflaged with bark and foliage to look like shelled stumps. If the enemy had not noticed the change to the scenery the next morning, then it was possible to climb up the pylons and quickly survey the scene in the hope of gaining useful information.

A French soldier in his bright blue uniform, which made them easy targets amongst the green and brown landscapes

A German officer in a camouflaged position in a wooded area of the Vosges

British soldiers moving forward through wire at the start of the Battle of the Somme, 1 July 1916

English SE-5
single-seater plane
(top) and a German
Rumpler two-seater
in aerial combat on
the British front

War in the Air

As World War I began just ten years after the first flight of a powered aeroplane, it may seem remarkable that they were developed sufficiently to be useful machines in the theatre of war. However, their evolution had been rapid, because they captured the public imagination. Aviators were frequently setting themselves new challenges to see what their flying machines could do, and this resulted in accelerated progress. By the time the war had started, the aeroplane was reliable and had begun to take on the fundamental form upon which modern machines are typically designed.

Initially, aeroplanes were put to use for the purpose of reconnaissance over land and sea. As the Western Front was situated on such flat terrain it was virtually impossible to gain a vantage point without being shot. The aeroplane had the advantage of being able to fly out of gun range and above enemy-held territory, so that it was possible to take photographs of enemy positions. Needless to say, both sides had the same idea, so the aeroplane quickly adapted from an observation device to a machine of war, able to attack other aircraft and defend itself from their attentions too.

A French-built Nieuport XXIII
reconnaissance plane, circa 1916

Many biplane and monoplane designs appeared, as engineers tried to keep their machines ahead in the arms race. Having machine guns became a vital component of these warplanes, but propellers presented an obstacle to the passage of bullets. Some designs had twin engines, to allow the guns to be mounted in between. Some had pushing propellers, to allow the guns to sit in front. Others had rear-mounted gunners to defend against attack from the rear. Eventually, a mechanism was invented to allow the machine gun to fire through the rotating propeller blades, which meant that dog-fights became a feature of airborne warfare.

A common problem with these early aeroplanes was that they had very little payload. They were simply not powerful and fast enough to lift much additional weight off the ground. This meant there was no possibility of carrying armour plating, so aircrew were always vulnerable to being hit by bullets from other aeroplanes and from the ground. It also meant that the concept of the aeroplane as a bomber was only in its infancy when the World War I ended. The concept of the fighter, however, was well and truly established.

Before the Royal Air Force existed in Britain, military airmen either belonged to the Royal Flying Corps, as part of the British Army, or the Royal Naval Air Service, as part of the Royal Navy. By April 1918, the potential of military aircraft had been fully accepted and both forces merged to create the RAF.

German flying ace Heinrich Gontermann stands near his Fokker DR-1 tri-plane on an airfield, Germany

British SE-5s locked in aerial combat, or dogfight, with German Fokker D7s

Belgian soldiers rush to commence battle,
on the banks of a canal near Ypres

Battles of Ypres

Fighting at the Western Front during World War I, was centred around a strategically important town, named Ypres, in West Flanders, which is a municipality of Belgium. During the course of the war, many offensives and defensives were fought along a frontline running roughly north-south. Although, there exact positions varied, many came to be known as the Battles of Ypres.

The first Battle of Ypres, in the autumn of 1914, established the pattern of trench warfare that would become synonymous with World War I. This was the result of some key factors. For one thing, many trained, regular soldiers perished in the hail of machine gun fire, so that they were replaced by volunteers. Also, reconnaissance information was lacking, which led to indecisive campaigns based largely on guesswork. As a consequence, both the Allies and the Germans found themselves losing personnel as quickly as they could be transported to the front, and a stalemate situation resulted.

In their individual shelters, on the front line, British soldiers, bayonet attached to their rifle barrel, await the German attack during the Battle of Ypres

Worst of all though, was the way in which the military was structured. The high command did not play an active role in the field. As a result, they kept sending lines of soldiers across no-man's-land, without appreciating that they were so easily cut down by enemy machine guns. Even though they were aware of such dreadfully high casualty rates, this lack of first-hand experience meant that it simply didn't impact them sufficiently to implement different tactics. The phrase 'going over the top' became part of the battlefield vernacular, as it was the command feared the most by the ordinary soldier, knowing it meant almost certain death. It also meant a pointless death, as it served no strategic purpose whatsoever.

Hundreds of thousands of Allies and Germans became casualties of war in Flanders, either killed, injured or missing in action. The exact numbers are not known, because records are imprecise. Astonishingly, nearly fifty thousand went missing during the Battles of Ypres. This is largely because they fell in no-man's-land and it was impossible to retrieve their corpses. Over time, shellfire either buried them or blew them to pieces, until there was no evidence of their having been there in the first place.

The endemic problem with the military high command's inability to empathize with the common man, was a result of the class structure in general society. Just as the Black Death caused a societal shift away from feudalism, due to the resulting lack of available manpower, so World War I would cause a similar societal shift away from the Victorian master-servant set-up. So, it can at least be said that the legacy of those who so needlessly died, was the initiation of a better society.

Stretcher bearers struggle in mud up to their knees to carry a wounded man to safety during the third battle of Ypres (Passchendaele)

British Soldiers in the Trenches during the Battle of Ypres in Belgium circa 1917

War at Sea

During World War I, warfare at sea played a significant factor, because it was all about supply of personnel and materials to and from other regions of the world. The Allies and the Central Powers both had substantial naval forces with which to do battle, but the Germans had developed the U-boat, which proved to be a particularly effective weapon against military vessels, merchant ships and troop carriers.

The U-boat (Underwater boat) was a class of submarine especially developed by the Germans for covert operations, able to fire torpedoes at the hulls of these craft with an element of surprise and devastation, which the Allies found difficult to counter. Sonar was yet to be invented and the British experimented with hydrophones in an effort to detect the engine noises of approaching U-boats with little success.

The role of the reconnaissance aeroplane became important as it was one of the best ways of detecting U-boats. It was then possible to alert shipping of their presence. The only effective way to counterattack U-boats was to drop depth charges and hope that the pressure waves would damage them sufficiently to either sink them or force them to the surface. For the most part though, it was better for cargo ships to travel in convoys, protected by military escorts. Until the introduction of escorts, U-boats had a field day sinking hundreds of supply ships bound for Britain and France from the US.

A British steamer is torpedoed, the picture was taken from the German U-Boat which has made the attack

Eventually the U-boats were rendered unable to sink sufficient numbers of Allied transport ships to have any serious effect on the supply chain to the frontline. The actions of U-boats against US warships also prompted the Americans to declare war on Germany, so the outcome of the war became inevitable.

As the U-boats are so well documented in history, it is often forgotten that the British had a number of World War I submarines of their own. They were primarily used in an effort to counter the U-boat threat, albeit with only limited success. The most numerous design was the E-class, of which 58 were launched between 1912 and 1916. They were also used to lay mines across shipping lanes used by the enemy and to assist in campaigns where troops needed to be delivered to coastal regions.

A U-boat opens fire with a deck cannon, on an allied merchant ship

The interior of a British E class submarine, 1916

Tanks

The Battle of the Somme was the first theatre of war in which a tank was used. The stalemate situation of trench warfare had arisen due to a peculiar combination of traditional tactics and advancing technology, which meant neither side was able to move forward in any decisive way. The idea behind the tank was simply a means of traversing the battlefield without being mown down by machine gun fire. It was a case of necessity being the mother of invention.

The first tanks were, however, only prototypes, as the Battle of the Somme was effectively their testing ground. They were unwieldy and unreliable, so that operators found them difficult to manoeuvre-especially under heavy fire-and would often find themselves stranded in no-man's-land, unable to restart their engines. In addition, they had poor visibility and limited effectiveness in terms of their own ability to return fire. This was because they had not yet adopted the standard tank format, with a rotating turret mounted above the traction unit. Instead, they had guns mounted to the side, between the track rails.

First World War tanks were descendants of vehicles like this early caterpillar-track farm machine

In short, tanks were primitive and poorly designed. As a concept though, their potential was clear enough, as they did indeed protect their occupants and they protected troops who used them as moving shields. In addition, they had a significant psychological effect on the enemy, who feared being crushed to death by the cumbersome machines as they trundled blindly over trenches and dug-outs.

The idea of the tank came from a British soldier named Ernest Dunlop Swinton. A friend had mentioned that an armoured tractor might be useful at the front, so Swinton began to think about ways of combining the basic concept of the track-propelled tractor, which had only just been invented, with a capacity to carry artillery.
The name 'tank' came about simply because the first machines were nothing more than mobile metal tanks. This early format, without the familiar gun turret, arose because the available technology was limited and it made sense to have everything contained within a single chamber and with a low centre of gravity.

By the close of World War I, the tank had begun to evolve rapidly. Ironically, it was the Germans who recognized its true potential and subsequently perfected its design between the wars. In 1940 the Panzer tanks used by the Germans, in their Blitzkrieg of Western Europe, were state-of-the-art machines that destroyed the tanks available to the Allies.

The German A7V tank, created by Daimler-Benz, weighed 26 tons and had a top speed of 12km/h; it carried a crew of up to 18 men

Zeppelins

Rigid airships, or dirigibles, were conceived in the late 19th century and the first flight took place in 1900, preceding the first powered aeroplane flight by three years. The name Zeppelin became synonymous with airships because it was the German pioneer Count Ferdinand von Zeppelin who got the idea off the ground, quite literally. Unlike hot air balloons, which relied on hot air being less dense than cold air, Zeppelins relied on the relative density of gases. They were filled with the lightweight gas hydrogen, which was less dense than the combination of gases in the atmosphere.

As Zeppelins could be made very large, it meant that they could carry considerable payloads, making them perfect for transporting passengers and their luggage. They could also be propelled with engines

and piloted, again unlike hot air balloons, so that regular services were established. Inevitably, the German military saw great potential in Zeppelins when World War I broke out. Zeppelins were ideal for scouting missions and for bombing the enemy.

They had a few drawbacks, as they were ill-suited to operating in windy weather conditions and hydrogen is highly flammable, taking only a spark to set it alight, but aeroplanes were simply not advanced enough to do a better job at that stage in history. So, Zeppelins were used extensively by the Germans, especially in situations that required prolonged reconnaissance work, such as detecting warships in the Baltic and North Sea. Aeroplanes simply did not have the range or fuel capacity to remain airborne for long enough.

A newspaper vendor in a London street announces the news of a Zeppelin raid on England

Zeppelins were even used for bombing raids over Britain, which came as quite a shock in a world coming to terms with the possibilities of flight in general. A number of east coast towns, cities and docks were targeted with success, not least because Britain was yet to implement a strategy against air raids. By 1916 many anti-aircraft guns and searchlights were positioned on British territory to counter the Zeppelin threat. In truth, the bombing raids did relatively little damage in material terms, but their psychological effect was considerable as no one had imagined that they might be in danger in their own homes when the frontline was hundreds of miles away in France.

This also called into question, whether it was ethically acceptable to bomb civilians. Inevitably, British sentiment towards the Germans grew increasingly negative, although the Kaiser did initially order that primary targets should be places of strategic value and that bombing in an indiscriminate manner simply to terrorize was to be avoided. As the war progressed, such considerations went out the window, and Zeppelins increasingly dropped bombs and incendiaries where they could. City defences improved however, so the airships began to target less densely populated places.

Belgian gun crew at work during
the Siege of Antwerp, 1914

Artillery

Trench warfare made rifles, pistols and machine guns relatively ineffective at reaching the enemy, unless they happened to attempt an assault or were foolish enough to expose themselves to gunfire. This meant that other field weapons were increasingly relied upon to strike at the unseen enemy. These weapons characteristically had parabolic trajectories so that the projectile came down from above and hopefully fell into enemy trenches.

The handheld grenade was designed for this very purpose, as it could be lobed in an arc, but it required the soldier to be near enough for the grenade to reach the target. This was virtually impossible as the soldier would need to leave his own trench and traverse no-man's-land to be within range. As a result, the mortar was developed, which was basically a mechanically assisted grenade. It was ejected from a launch tube and was capable of travelling several hundred yards.

A German L21 Zeppelin sinks off
the coast of Yarmouth, Norfolk,
after having been shot down

Three 8-inch howitzers of 39th Siege Battery, Royal Garrison Artillery (RGA), firing from the Fricourt-Mametz Valley during the Battle of the Somme

Belgian soldiers make a charge near the River Yser

Next on the scale were the field guns. They were capable of firing exploding shells over several miles distance, so they were stationed a long way behind the frontline in order that their ammunition fell on the enemy at the correct angle to do maximum damage. Needless to say, the room for error was considerable, so accurate sighting adjustments relied greatly on reconnaissance information. Even then, the targeting could be quite arbitrary, so the big guns kept firing until they had given the whole area a good pounding. Of course, it was also possible to be hit by friendly fire, if the artillerymen set their guns with too short a range.

The most frequently used artillery were howitzers. They were short barrelled guns that fell somewhere between mortars and field guns in terms of their firepower and their trajectory. They were also relatively lightweight and mobile, making them ideally suited to being moved about behind the field of battle. As howitzers were designed to fire ammunition over relatively short distances, at high trajectories, they were capable of delivering shells twice the size of those delivered by equivalent field guns.

The combination of the steep angle of attack and large shell size made them formidable weapons when they hit target. If a battery of howitzers launched a simultaneous attack, then whole areas containing enemy positions could be obliterated in minutes. The aim was to breach the enemy's frontline in this way, so that offensives could quickly be launched before the enemy had time to recover and defend themselves. This usually worked for only short periods of time, so that the Western Front changed shape here and there, but essentially remained in the same place year after year.

Gallipoli Campaign

With Russia as part of the Entente, along with Britain and France, it was in the Allies' interests to have a sea route from the Mediterranean to Russia. This meant having to secure part of the Ottoman Empire, so that safe passage could be made through the Sea of Marmara to the Black Sea, via the Bosphorus. In order to achieve this, a force was sent to seize the Gallipoli peninsula, so that the Dardanelles strait would be under Allied control. Then, the Allied force would continue eastward to take the city of Constantinople (Istanbul), thereby completing the objective. At least, that was the plan. As it turned out, things went disastrously wrong.

Due to Allied commitments at the Western Front, only a small naval expeditionary force was dispatched to invade the peninsula. The terrain was difficult and led to an initial withdrawal. By the time a larger force arrived, the element of surprise had been wasted and the Turks had amassed a considerable force ready to defend their territory. As a result, the Allies found themselves pinned along the coast with the Turks holding the higher ground inland. Both sides continued feeding in reinforcements, but the frontline remained more-or-less frozen.

British troops of the IX Corps on the beach after landing at Suvla on the Aegean coast of the Gallipoli peninsula in Turkey

Dreadnoughts bombard the heights of Chocolate Hill and Lalu Baba and cover our advance from Suvla Bay, Gallipoli, Turkey

After nine months of ferocious hostilities, the Allies finally decided to cut their losses in December 1915, and withdraw. They had lost over 70,000 men, while the Turks had lost about 60,000. It was one of the most costly campaigns of World War I and achieved nothing except to highlight just how wasteful modern warfare could be. Over 11,000 of the Allied losses were ANZAC (Australian and New Zealand Army Corp). They had travelled half way around the world, only to be slaughtered.

Weather conditions on the Gallipoli peninsula made life particularly difficult for the Allies. In the summer it grew unbearably hot, so that corpses decomposed very rapidly and the smell of putrefying flesh filled the air. In the winter it grew unbearably cold, with flash floods filling trenches and drowning troops. The general lack of hygiene also resulted in outbreaks of dysentery. With no prospect of a successful outcome to the campaign, morale fell so low that evacuation was the only option left available.

Turkish troops on parade at Gallipoli, 1915

The Battle of the Somme

The Somme is a river in north-eastern France, just south of Flanders in Belgium. The word 'somme' is derived from the Celtic for tranquillity, which is about as ironic as anything can possibly be. Ironic, because in terms of human loss of life, the Battle of the Somme was one of the most costly of all time, with over a million killed between 1st July and 18th November 1916. The banks of the Somme were anything but tranquil for those tragic weeks and the battle changed the public perception of war forever, because so many families were affected in such a short space of time.

The original intention behind the offensive that marked the beginning of the Battle of the Somme, was for the Allies to punch a hole through the German frontline and attempt to bring the war to a conclusion. However, the Germans proved to be a formidable enemy and prevented a breach from occurring. The battle then developed into a slanging match of countless attacks and counterattacks, so that fighting became contained within a particular area only a few miles wide and about fifteen miles long.

Canadian troops prepare for the charge over the top at the Battle of the Somme, 1916

Although the Somme frontline moved insufficiently to justify the vast numbers of casualties, it is now considered to have been a pivotal battle in World War I, because attrition to the German army was considerable and led to a retreat a couple of months later to the Hindenburg line, some forty miles east. Whereas the Allies were able to reinforce their forces following the battle, the Germans were not, so they had suffered a damaging blow.

The tragedy is that it took so many lives, on both sides, to achieve the necessary bias in strength for the Allies to get the upper hand. The same result could have been achieved by sending the million soldiers home to their families. But that is where World War I differed from past conflicts. Traditionally, armies were more representative of populations rather than comprising such a high percentage of the populations themselves. As a consequence, battles were fought more like games of chess, in a chosen location on a certain day, to determine the winner. As a result, relatively few lost their lives to the ritual. Modern warfare had become an unnecessary cull of those who were needed to maintain the infrastructure of society when hostilities ceased.

A German soldier wearing a gas mask about to hurl a hand-grenade from a trench during The Battle of the Somme

Roll call of the 1st Battalion, Lancashire Fusiliers on the afternoon of 1 July 1916, following their assault on Beaumont Hamel, Battle of the Somme

War-horses, War-dogs and War-pigeons

Perhaps due to the enormous human cost of World War I, it is often forgotten that many animals died in the conflict too. Of course, large areas of natural habitat were turned to fields of mud and laced with poisonous chemicals, so many wild animals would have perished as a result, but here we consider the domesticated animals used by the armed forces in the war effort.

It is reckoned that about half a million war-horses died in the service of both the Allies and the Central Powers. As tracked vehicles, such as tanks and gun tractors, were only introduced and developed during the war, it meant that horses were still the best way of carrying and pulling equipment over uneven terrain. They were also very effective transportation for personnel, either on horseback, as cavalry, on in troop wagons. Horses therefore played an important role at the Western Front while the front lines were fluid and mobile.

When the trench warfare began, horses took a supporting role, working between the supply heads and the back trenches, to ensure that ammunition, foodstuffs and other provisions found their way to those who needed them.

On the Eastern Front, where entrenchment was less frequent, horses continued to play a central role in the military movements of the Russians and the Austro-Hungarians. It should be remembered also, that there were few roads in Eastern Europe, so the horse was a vital mode of transport and traction over rough country.

French Lancers on horseback follow up a German retreat

French troops with dogs, 1916

Incredibly, about a million war-dogs lost their lives in
World War I. They were used to carry messages at the
Western Front, and in other frontline zones, where
it was too dangerous for humans to risk exposing
themselves. Portable radio systems were not yet
available, so a physical means of delivering messages
was essential. As a result, the dogs were actively
targeted by the enemy to prevent the communications
from reaching their intended destinations.
Messages would be inserted in canisters secured
to the dogs' collars.

For long-distance communications, thousands of war-
pigeons were used.
Having been kept in pigeon lofts at headquarters, they
would use their homing instincts to return to those
lofts when released in the field. Messages would be
inserted into tubes attached to the pigeons' legs. As
pigeons are quite swift flyers they stood a reasonable
chance of returning without being shot from the skies.
Many British homing pigeons flew from Belgium and
France to England. It became illegal to shoot pigeons
for sport or food, in case they happened to be winged
messengers. Also, many peregrine falcons were shot
to prevent them from hunting the pigeons en route.

British soldiers in the south of England
train a carrier pigeon to deliver
messages during World War I

Hindenburg Line

K nown at the time as the Siegfried Line, but now known as the Hindenburg Line, to avoid confusion with a similar boundary in World War II, it was a fortified line of retreat prepared by the Germans as a precautionary measure, just in case they found themselves in a situation where they needed to lick their wounds. As it turned out, the Battle of the Somme depleted the Germans so much that they had no choice but to give up a forty mile swathe of territory in order to fall back.

The Hindenburg Line was a string of fortifications and tank barriers, designed to keep the Allies at bay while the Germans regrouped and replenished their forces. The Germans had a shortage of manpower because they were fighting on two fronts and this is what compromised them into retreat. Added to this, they had problems with the supply of equipment and munitions. Many soldiers with engineering skills were returned to the German industrial regions in an effort to improve production. In the meantime, the remaining German army had to defend the Hindenburg Line until the situation improved.

Wounded Canadian soldiers within the Hindenburg Line are being taken back from the firing lines by captured German prisoners

A section of a Hindenburg trench near Cologne Farm

The British had, themselves, experienced as shortage of shells known as the Shell Crisis in 1915, which resulted in political reforms to ensure that the entire British economy was geared towards the war effort. New factories were built and labour forces recruited to manufacture adequate numbers of shells and the materials needed.

Eventually the fortunes of the Germans seemed to be improving, when Eastern Front hostilities died away due to civil unrest within Russia. The Communists took control in 1917 and it wasn't in their interests to continue fighting the war, because they had their own civil war to deal with. This meant that the Central Powers found themselves able to redeploy redundant forces along the Western Front and once again push westward away from the Hindenburg Line.

However, the Germans had provoked the USA into declaring war by this juncture and US troops had begun pouring into Europe, ready to join the war effort. As a result, the Germans simply could not muster sufficient resources to counter the influx of Allied support. The writing was on the wall for the Germans and the Hindenburg Line came to represent their Achilles' heel during the interwar years. That is why crossing the Hindenburg Line became so symbolic for Adolf Hitler during his invasion of Western Europe in 1940.

Balloons

When the Western Front had settled into trench warfare, the most immediate problem was acquiring intelligence about what the enemy was up to. For the Germans, this wasn't such a problem, because they had established their positions on what little high ground there was available. These hills were not large, but they gave the Germans a considerable advantage when all around was so flat, as they could observe the Allies.

Aeroplanes were used to make reconnaissance flyovers, but there was always the risk of having them shot from the air and they were expensive to keep in the air for long periods of time. For this reason, balloons were developed by the Allies and the Germans, to enable prolonged observation of activities across no-man's-land.

These observation balloons were filled with either hydrogen or coal gas (a gas mixture) to make them lighter than air. They had to be tethered to the ground by ropes or cables to prevent them from blowing away with the wind, so they were kept well behind the frontline, out of the range of enemy fire. Observers were suspended from baskets below the balloons and communicated with the ground via telephone lines, which hung down.

A German observation balloon is filled with gas, 1915

A number of balloon designs were developed to provide stability for the observers, so that they weren't forever spinning and changing direction. The Allies favoured the kite balloon, while the Germans favoured the drachen (dragon) balloon. Both had a front end and a tail, so that they would sit still with the prevailing wind and allow the observers to do their job. In order to keep them taut on their guy-wires, the balloons were fitted with pockets to catch the breeze, in a similar way to the sails on a yacht.

On a good day, with sufficient altitude and clear conditions, observers could see usefully for twenty or thirty miles, which was especially useful for instructing artillery batteries in adjusting their howitzers and field guns.

Due to the risk of being hit by artillery shells, the balloon operators were the first to make routine use of parachutes. The packed parachute had not been invented, so aeroplane crews had no means of escape, but observation balloons had hung parachutes, ready for immediate use.

Barrage balloons were also devised during World War I, but they were not used in theatres of battle. Instead, they were used in cities in an effort to prevent aircraft from making bombing raids. They were unmanned balloons that carried cables to deter aircraft, but they were only effective at relatively low altitudes, because the cables were heavy to lift.

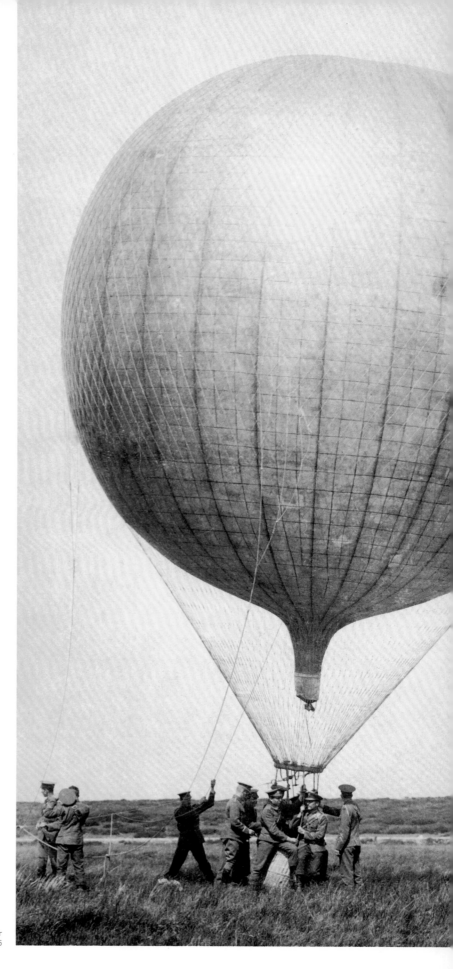

The launch of a hot-air balloon used for reconnaissance, 1915

Trench Design

In typical warfare, trenches are temporary structures, occupied for a few hours or a few days at most. On the Western Front, the situation was entirely different, as trenches were occupied for weeks, months or even years. As a result, their design was rather more considered, from a number of viewpoints. From an offensive point of view, trenches needed to provide soldiers with places to fire weapons and points where it was possible to leave the front of the trench to mount assaults across no-man's-land. From a defensive point of view, trenches needed to protect soldiers from enemy gun and shell fire, and make it difficult for raiding parties to mount effective attacks.

Long-term trenches also needed to be stable, to ensure that the sides didn't collapse. They also needed to include billets, where soldiers could eat and sleep when off-duty. In addition, there was the matter of ablutions and sanitation. In other words, trenches needed to cater for day-to-day requirements of their human occupants over long periods of time.

Trenches were usually equipped with duck-boarding on the ground, to provide an even and dry surface for the soldiers' feet. Wooden shuttering was also used on the sides of trenches to provide stability, and to form the walls and roofs of dug-outs and toilets. Frontline trenches would often include alcoves and bends, so that raiders were unable to simply jump in one end and fire their guns along the entirety of the trench and kill the occupants.

A trench in the low flat country
near La Bassee Villa, 1917

Many trenches were designed as a system, to allow the rotation of personnel. A central gallery trench, running towards the frontline, would have perpendicular trenches radiating outwards on either side. Typically, there would be frontline trenches, support-line trenches and reserve-line trenches, so that a community of soldiers would take it in turns to carry out different duties. The central gallery trench was heavily defended, because it was the conduit between all other trenches.

All-in-all, life in the trenches was pretty miserable. As well as the constant threat of death, conditions were perpetually dirty and unhygienic, so it was essential that soldiers were given time away from the frontline, to raise their spirits and lift their morale. A number of entertainment troupes were sent to the Western Front for this purpose. They would put on amusing shows to encourage troops to laugh, relax and socialize. Having their minds distracted from the daily horrors of warfare was considered to be vital therapy.

A deserted trench in Ypres, Belgium, site of three World War I battles

Medicine

Disease and infection were responsible for more death in World War I than any other cause. Squalid, unsanitary conditions on the Western Front, the Eastern Front and the Ottoman Front made the likelihood of contracting ailments very high.

Antibiotics had not been discovered, so bacterial infections were a serious problem. Communicable bacterial illnesses, such as tuberculosis, dysentery, typhus and cholera would spread rapidly due to a general lack of hygiene and the close proximity of the combatants. Similarly all battle wounds, large and small, had the potential to become infected, simply because the environment was filled with bacteria. Pieces of rotting cadaver and faeces littered the earth surrounding the trenches. In addition, there were pests, such as rats, flies, fleas and lice, which carried bacteria around with them.

Three German soldiers display rats killed in their trench the previous night, 1916

Many injuries became gangrenous with bacterial infection. The flesh dies (necrosis), leading to blood poising (septicaemia) and then death. Without antibiotics, the only available treatment was to cut the dead tissue away or amputate limbs so that the remaining flesh was free of infection and stood a reasonable chance of healing. Of course, the success of this surgery in turn relied on keeping the newly exposed tissue free from further infection, with the use of disinfectants and dressings. In the field, this was by no means easy to achieve.

Surviving combat injuries was very much a matter of the nature of the injury and its location on the body. Head and body injuries were far more likely to end in death than injuries to the arms and legs. Also, shrapnel injuries tended to be worse than bullet injuries, because the fragments of shell would rip through the flesh, causing considerable damage. Dirty debris would also be introduced to body,

because shells exploded on contact with the ground. Penetrating injuries were always difficult because of the difficulty in removing the foreign bodies and then ensuring that the wound was sterile.

When daily hostilities ceased, stretchers would be used to carry the injured away from the battlefield. The stretcher bearers would be protected from enemy fire by wearing the Red Cross symbol, which was recognized and respected as a sign of benevolence. The injured would then be taken on to field hospitals, which were large tents filled with beds. If there injuries were minor, then they would be treated and send back to the front as soon as possible. If their injuries were more serious, then they would be treated and then sent to proper hospitals farther afield, so that the field hospitals had available beds for new casualties.

A wounded soldier has a bandage wrapped around his face as he receives first aid treatment, 1918

Helping a wounded English
soldier on the front in 1915

Officers versus other ranks in a football match played by members of the 26th Divisional Ammunition Train near their camp, just outside the city of Salonika, Christmas Day, 25 December 1915

Keeping Human

Vital to maintaining the sanity of World War I combatants, whether on land, at sea or in the air, were the small things that meant so much. The postal service was an essential part of the war effort as it allowed loved ones to stay in touch by letter when they were parted for long periods of time and there was a good chance they would never meet again. Much of what historians now know about the human side of the war comes from the letters sent during those years. Most surviving soldiers either chose not to discuss the war, or simply were unable too because it was too emotive. The things they had witnessed were best forgotten for the sake of pursuing a happier life, so the way they achieved this was by trying not to think about it. Over time, they put distance between themselves and their memories. Only in old age, did they feel ready to recount their experiences, motivated by their desire to make sure the world did not forget the enormous sacrifice.

In order to while away the time in between periods of action, men would play card and board games. Nearly everyone smoked in those days, so any form of tobacco was highly valued. Regular soldiers were given a two ounce ration of tobacco per week on the Western Front. Other rations included corned or bully beef, bacon, cheese, sugar, tea, jam, bread, biscuits, condiments, vegetables and rum. Germans rations were much the same, although they included cigars, coffee and snuff.

The Early Years

As Winston Churchill and Adolf Hitler were young men during World War I, it is worth considering their involvement to understand how they became the men they were in World War II.

At the outbreak of World War I, Winston Churchill was already a high profile military and political figure. He had been First Lord of the Admiralty since 1911 and introduced a number of important modernizing reforms. However, it was Churchill's idea to mount the disastrous Gallipoli Campaign, so he was forced to resign in 1915. Faced with having to rebuild his reputation, Churchill became an officer at the Western Front, where he took a proactive role and exposed himself to considerable danger. He had exhibited similar reckless daring at the Second Boer War some fifteen years before and it was this fearlessness and determination that would eventually lead the British people to put their faith in him during World War II.

Winston Churchill and General French walk their horses
together on manoeuvres during World War I

Adolf Hitler dressed in his field uniform during World War I

Unlike Churchill, Adolf Hitler was yet to make a name for himself when World War I began. He volunteered to serve the German army and became a dispatch runner, seeing action in a number of major battles, including Ypres, the Somme, Arras and Passchendaele. For his bravery and injuries he was awarded the Iron Cross, Second Class in 1914 and First Class in 1918. Having invested so much enthusiasm and effort into the war, he was incensed when the Central Powers capitulated to the Entente and this catalyzed his nationalist ideology that would evolve into Nazism.

Intriguingly, Churchill and Hitler had similarities. They were both attracted to danger as an expression of machismo and both had forged reputations based on those experiences. Also, they both fancied themselves as artists and were competent amateurs at drawing and painting. The difference was that Hitler had wanted to become a professional artist, while to Churchill it was a cathartic pastime.

Both men were certainly egotists, but they came from very different backgrounds and that made them very different as personalities. Churchill came from the British upper class and had a sense of entitlement and expectation, which is why he bent and broke the rules with impunity. Hitler had to climb the social ladder and deal with a fundamental sense of inferiority, which gave him his passion and drive to succeed, but also riddled him with hatred and prejudices. In power, Churchill saw himself honestly, as a flawed leader doing his best for his people. Hitler portrayed himself as a divinely chosen and faultless leader, but underneath he knew the truth, which is why he took his own life when he realized the unlikely game was up.

Corporal Adolf Hitler, right, with two other soldiers and a dog during his stay in a military hospital, WWI, Pasewalk, Pomerania

Trench Raids and Weapons

Due to the loggerhead of trench warfare at the Western Front, soldiers were unable to advance. Day time assaults were suicidal, as the soldiers were cut down by machine gun fire as soon as they went over the top. As a result, night time raids became the modus operandi on both sides.

The objective was to black-up with burnt cork and cross no-man's-land undetected and then enter the enemy trench and dispatch as many of the foe as possible without being heard. This meant that noisy firearms were not to be used, unless their cover was blown and it made no difference. So hand weapons, such as bayonets, trench knives, Bowie knives and knuckle-dusters, were all used and rifles and pistols were kept in reserve.

The principal strategy was to catch sentries by surprise and stab them through the heart or cut their throats, whilst preventing them from shouting out and alerting others. Once the sentries were dealt with, it was then possible to raid billets, simply by lobbing grenades inside and making a quick exit to avoid being caught in the explosion and to escape before reserve soldiers arrived. So, the initial stage of a raid would be silent, but followed by the chaos of explosions and gunfire.

A British soldier in a flooded dug-out in a front line trench near Ploegsteert Wood, Flanders, 1917

With any luck, the raiders would make it back across no-man's-land to live another day, but there was always the risk of being caught on barbed wire or being shot by friendly fire. In an effort to eliminate the possibility of being mistaken for the enemy, raiders used passwords in order to let their own sentries know who they were in the darkness.

Periscopes were often used by sentries to keep an eye on no-man's-land without the risk of being shot. If they suspected a raid might be immanent then flares would be fired to illuminate the sky and expose the raiders, so that machine gunners could see their target and open fire.

This tit-for-tat raiding was an on-going part of trench warfare and was encouraged by high command, because it prevented soldiers from losing their combative edge. The constant risk of being killed and challenge of having to kill, kept the troops psychologically tuned for the job in hand, in readiness for eventual movement in the frontline.

Two British soldiers waiting for the signal to attack at Ginchy, 1916

The Flying Aces

As World War I progressed, so did mechanization in the air. It wasn't long before fighter aeroplanes were manoeuvrable and reliable enough to partake in aerial dog-fights. The aeroplanes did not yet pose a significant threat to ground operations, except in a reconnaissance role, so pilots were waging a private battle for air superiority, partly motivated by the intelligence threat but also as a matter of pride.

Aeroplanes were conspicuous and they captured the imagination in a way unlike other machines of war. As a result, they possessed propaganda value and the pilots were regarded as courageous and romantic daredevils. In this rarefied atmosphere, the phenomenon of the flying ace was born and much exploited by the media of the era, on both sides. The flying ace came to personify the war effort from both the Allied and German perspectives, because the public was able to see a face and read a name, which represented all of those fighting at the Front.

A Sopwith Camel, 1917; being small and lightweight, represented the latest in fighter design at the time

German fighter triplane Fokker Dr 1, plane of the Baron Manfred von Richthofen (The Red Baron)

Probably the most famous of all flying aces is Manfred von Richthofen, who went by the sobriquet Red Baron. This was because he flew a distinctive bright-red Fokker Dr.1 triplane. He chalked up eighty air combat victories, before being killed by enemy fire whilst in the air near the Somme in April 1918. He had a brother, Lothar von Richthofen, who was also a flying ace, with forty victories to his name by the end of the war. Both were handsome and decorated young men, making them very popular with the Teutonic public. Other notable German flying aces include Oswald Boelcke (40 victories) and Max Immelman (15 victories).

The German approach to keeping tallies of air combat victories was far more formal than that of the Allies, which probably said something about their ordered and serious approach to life in general. British, French, Italian and US flying aces were recognized, but they were celebrated more modestly and their victory tally records are more vague, as if it were not all that important. What mattered was that they had five or more kills, as that was sufficient to demonstrate that they had prowess at the controls. After all, many pilots only lasted a few flights before being shot from the skies or crashing, so anyone who managed to both stay alive and kill a few Huns was a hero regardless of tally.

A concentration camp for German prisoners of war in Surrey

Prisoners of War

During the course of World War I, many combatants found themselves captured by the enemy and held in POW (Prisoner Of War) camps. In all, about seven million were incarcerated between 1914 and 1918. As housing and feeding prisoners was an inconvenience and expensive, both in terms of resources and manpower, most prisoners of war were treated with general disdain and kept in squalid conditions with all expenses spared.

European nations had signed the Hague Convention in 1907, which stipulated that prisoners of war were to be treated humanely and that they were prisoners of the government, not the people. This was important, as it made it clear that the government would be held accountable for any inhumane treatment and torture. All of the main participating nations in World War I had signed the convention, except for the Turks, as the Ottoman Empire was part of Asia.

The Germans kept just short of a quarter of a million Allied prisoners in about three-hundred POW camps. Conditions were typically harsh, as the Central Powers could ill-afford to divert much of their war effort to maintaining and guarding the camps. The officers and guards tended to be old or second-rate soldiers, who were not fit for duty at the frontlines. All aspects of prison life made the experience a test of endurance. Food was poor, sanitation was unhygienic, space was limited and so on. This made the environment such that physical and mental illnesses were commonplace.

The prisoners were, however, allowed to send and receive letters from home, which was an important psychological catharsis and gave them something to focus on. The Red Cross provided modest rations, but these were insufficient to sustain health and life, so the prisoners relied on a lifeline of food parcels sent by their loved ones.

A number of escapes and escape attempts occurred. Although there was the obvious benefit of being freed from prison conditions, many soldiers, especially officers, had a strong sense of duty and wanted to return to active service. Planning escapes also gave them something to think about to alleviate the tedium, and there was the additional satisfaction in knowing that escapes cost the Germans valuable time and effort in searching for them even if they failed to remain liberated.

Prisoners were also used to perform many kinds of work to assist in the war effort against their own people. As the war dragged on, the Central Powers had a drastic shortage of manpower, so the prison labour force became vitally important. Following the ceasefire on the Eastern Front, the Russians POWs were not released, because Germany could not afford to let go of any assistance in the renewed war effort on the Western Front.

A German officer
tying up a Russian
prisoner of war, 1916

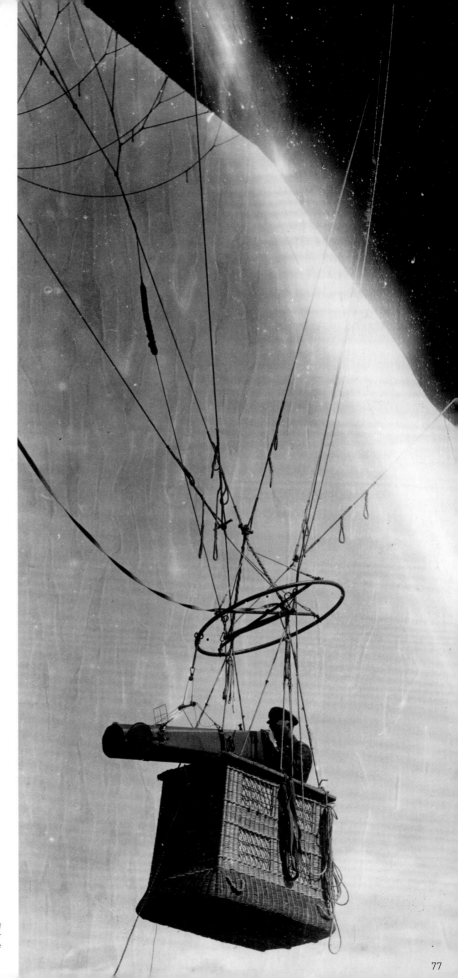

A German observer in the basket of
a hot-air balloon using a camera for
aerial reconnaissance

Intelligence and Espionage

At the frontline in World War I, reconnaissance was the way most intelligence about the enemy was gathered. This was simply using vantage points, observation balloons, aeroplanes and so on to spy on the enemy's movements. This was done covertly if at all possible, so that the enemy was unaware that it had been compromised. But, overt spying was also practiced, when aircraft would fly over and take photographs, for example.

Trench codes were also used at the Western Front, so that important information didn't fall into enemy hands during trench raids. The only problem was, that code books were required to decipher incoming messages and to compose outgoing messages. This meant that code books would need to be very well hidden, or codes would need to be periodically changed. As a result, those at the front were often reluctant to bother with codes even though high command considered it a good idea. It was simply a difference in opinion over the practicality of using codes in real situations , where the perceived advantages could be lost by the time and inconvenience.

Away from the Front, espionage was rife on both sides, because it was useful to know about the bigger picture, such as major troop movements, supply routes and weapons' manufacture. For this reason, all participating nations had agents whose job it was to gather information and relay it back to those for whom it was useful. This led to double-agents too, who posed as friends but were actually working for the enemy by providing disinformation.

One of the most famous suspected agents was a woman called Mata Hari, a celebrated Dutch burlesque dancer, whose real name was Margaretha Zelle. Being Dutch, she was neutral and able to cross borders during the war, which she did frequently and was consequently questioned by the British counter-espionage team. She was first suspected of working for the French, but then information came to light that implicated her as a German agent. When she went to trial the prosecution could not conclusively prove her guilt, but they stated that she was very likely to be responsible for the deaths of fifty thousand troops. As a result she was executed by firing squad in October 1917, under the rationale that she was probably guilty anyway, and that her publicized death would serve as a sober reminder of the seriousness of furnishing the enemy with intelligence. These days her trial would have collapsed, but the scandal happened at a crucial juncture in the war, when people were getting very weary of the rising death toll and looking for someone to blame.

Reconnaissance in the gorges of the Rajec, An infantry sergeant observing the Prilep road from the Drenovo Pass, Serbia

Admission, Abdication and Armistice

By late September 1918, it dawned upon the German high-command that the war at the Western Front was unwinnable. The hollow victory at the Eastern Front, due to the civil war in Russia, had been used by propagandists to make the German people think that victory at the Western Front was now an inevitable conclusion. In truth, the renewed effort in the west was too little too late. By that time, the Germans were critically short of manpower and resources, and they had provoked the US into joining the Allies. Despite their initial success at moving the frontline by implementing new tactics, they were a spent force and the tide had turned against them.

On the 29th of September, Kaiser Wilhelm II received a communication from General Ludendorff recommending a ceasefire in anticipation that the Allies would soon break through the German lines and take the front eastward to Germany. By 5th October, Germany had asked to negotiate peace with the Allies, but the conditions, including the Kaiser's abdication and withdrawal to the German border, were considered too harsh, so Ludendorff had a change of heart.

By late October, revolution was in the air, as factions of the German military were beginning to turn against the monarchy in favour of a democratic government. As the situation escalated, the Kaiser was forced to abdicate by his own people and the Weimar Republic was announced on the 9th of November. Negotiations with the Allies were concluded at 5 am on the morning of the 11th of November, with the armistice to come into effect at 11am to provide enough time for the word to spread along the Western Front.

Crowds of people celebrating the signing by Germany of the armistice on November 11, 1918

Newspapers report the abdication of William II, emperor of Germany, November 10, 1918

From the point of view of the German military, the war had come to a premature end due to the political revolution. Largely unaware that the political revolution had actually been a symptom of German attrition, they felt as if they had been prevented from fighting a war they were about to win, so their pride was deeply hurt and they sought people to blame. It was this sense of unfinished business that would prevail in the interwar years and give Adolf Hitler the platform upon which he would build the Nazi cause.

For a while, the new government of Germany was communist, and this is why Hitler was so anti-communist. His subjective view of the armistice made him believe that the communists were to blame for bringing the war to a close and preventing the Germans from having their glorious victory. Had he apprehended that the underlying cause was poor administration of finite German resources, then he might not have allowed history to repeat itself with his own blinkered strategic decisions during World War II.

Excited London citizens cheering in streets and from atop double decker bus after news of the World War I armistice signing is heard

Tyne Cot Cemetery, the largest Commonwealth war
grave cemetery in the world, near Ypres, Belgium

The Socio-political Legacy

If we are to find something positive in the
wholesale slaughter of World War I, then it is
best to consider the revolutions and reforms
that it catalyzed in Europe and elsewhere in the
world. Above all else, it prompted the rise of the
common man in society, simply because so many
had made the ultimate sacrifice and so many
families were left affected by the war in one way
or another.

In Britain, the erosion of the class system had been
initiated and voting reforms allowed the masses to
have a much greater say in who should be elected
to government. Significantly, women over the age
of thirty were also allowed to vote for the first time
in the post-war election of December 1918. British
suffragettes had been actively campaigning before
the war, but had agreed to contribute to the war
effort in 1915 when it became apparent that the
conflict was going to last for some time.

Due to the loss of so many young men, there was also a shortage of manpower in post-war Britain. This marked a social change, because those available to work had a greater say in terms of pay, working conditions and prospects for promotion. In effect, this ushered in the true middle-class, as Britain became a meritocracy, allowing people to climb the social ladder according to their skills and abilities. Prior to that, people very much belonged to the class in which they were born, so relatively few had the opportunity or wherewithal to become upwardly mobile.

Another aspect of the legacy of World War I was the early signs of empire disintegration. Many British colonies had taken part in the conflict and lost considerable numbers of people, yet there was no perceivable gain to be had from it. As a result, the seeds of independence were sown, because those populations realized that they would be better off governing themselves and making their own decisions. The brave new world was just around the corner.

Meanwhile, Russia was undergoing its transformation into a communist nation. The royal family had all been executed and the Bolsheviks had taken control under Lenin. The general Russian population had enough of living in poverty, while the aristocracy lived in luxury. Due to the interrelatedness of the European royal families, the inclusion of Russia in World War I had seemed like a cosying gesture on the part of the Tsar and Russian society was ripe for political revolution.

British POWs being given refreshments on a London railway platform on their arrival back in Britain

The picture shows the revolutionists on the second day of the Russian Revolution

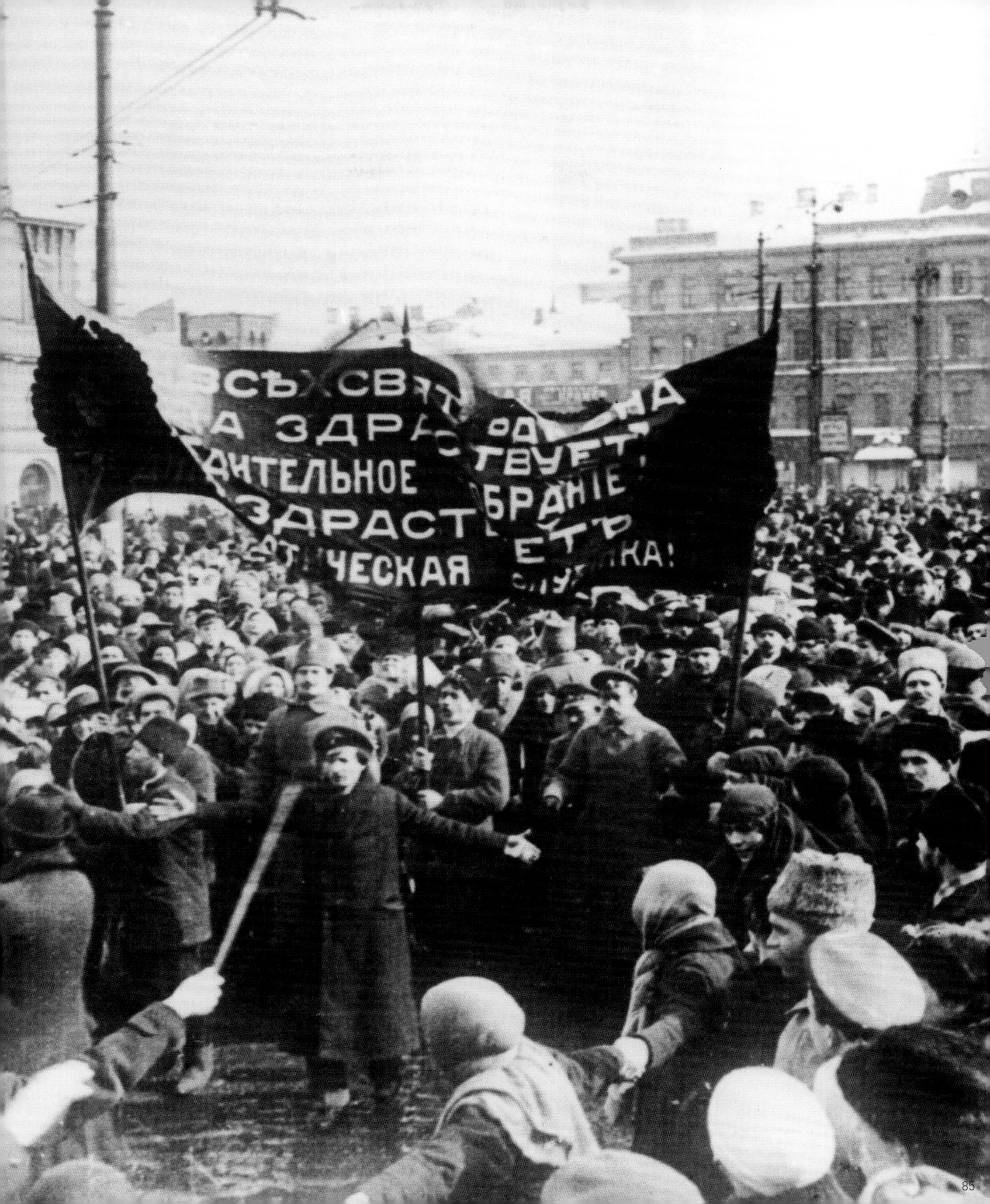

French Prime Minister Georges Clemenceau (left), US President Woodrow Wilson (centre) and British Prime Minister David Lloyd-George (far right) leaving the Palace of Versailles after signing the Treaty of Versailles, Paris, 28th June 1919

The Ember Left Glowing

General John Pershing, who led the American Expeditionary Force in World War I, was very much against the idea of an armistice with Germany. He wanted to defeat the German army in no uncertain terms and warned that the Germans would only rise again if allowed to think that the war ended in a draw. So it was, that an ember was left glowing in the ashes, ready to be fanned back into flames.

The terms agreed for the armistice, which was officially signed at the Treaty of Versailles on 28th June 1919, were quite harsh on the Germans, to ensure that they were rendered unable to launch any new offensives. The result was economic collapse in post-war Germany and this only served to nurture resentment towards the Allied powers.

By 1920 the Nationalist Socialist Workers' (Nazi) Party had been established in Germany to counter the communist movement, held to account for the state of the nation at that time. Adolf Hitler became leader of the party in 1921 and happened to possess a gift for public speaking that captured the imaginations of many disillusioned Germans, who were seduced by the idea of Germany rising once again.

German dictator Adolf Hitler on board a ferry in the Baltic Sea, 1921

Adolf Hitler addresses
soldiers with his back
facing the camera at a
Nazi rally in Dortmund,
Germany, 1933

Hitler saluting at a Nuremberg rally, 1934

In addition, Hitler had developed resentment for Jews, because they seemed to be well of in relation to the rest of the population, but kept their wealth to themselves and were disinclined to show benevolence. Thus, Hitler had his targets for vilification, which he would use to whip up a frenzy of hatred and blame. Communists and Jews were to be the pariahs of the German nation, enabling Hitler to provide his followers with a collective focus for their frustrations, which actually had nothing to do with the truth but served as a very effective political tool.

In order to give the Germans a sense of behavioural cohesion, the Nazis also introduced notions of Aryan purity and perfection by educating the young with quasi-Darwinian ideas. This led to the additional persecution of anyone who didn't fit with the ideal. The physically disabled, the mentally ill and those from other races and religions were all on the list of undesirables.

Between 1918 and 1939, Germany had lifted itself from its knees and resolved to restore its own pride by once again attempting to conquer Europe. Pershing's prophecy had come true, only this time it came with a far more dangerous ideology that brainwashed the German army into believing it belonged to the master race. In the end though, it would be that delusion of superiority that would lead to the fall of the Third Reich.

WORLD WAR TWO

Let Us Go Forward Together
(Churchill) an iconic WWII poster

A news boy selling the News
Of The World carries a poster
proclaiming Britain's declaration
of war on Germany, 1939

An American soldier from 7th
Armored Division mans the
machine gun of his tank while
on manoeuvres, 1942

The Build-up to War

In the years preceding World War II it was evident that Germany had military ambitions, simply because of the rhetoric used by Adolf Hitler. There was also a considerable increase in the manufacture of arms and machines of war, as well as the active recruitment of young men into the Nazi Party and German forces. However, politicians in other European countries had the naïve idea that avoiding conflict was a matter diplomacy. They invested a great deal of time and effort into visiting Hitler, thinking that he would be swayed by their good will. In fact, they were making the mistake of judging him by their own standards, for the truth was that Hitler had every intention of putting his plans of conquest into action regardless of these gestures. He was merely pulling the wool over their eyes as he prepared for all-out warfare. When the time was right, Hitler simply got on with what he had always intended, confident that nothing and no one could stop him.

A similar situation had arisen in Japan. There too, military resources were being amassed to set the wheels of territorial ambition in motion. With the Japanese emperor on the throne, the regime itself didn't need a particular personality to take the lead, but the intent was clear.
As the Japanese already had a foothold in Manchuria, they had a pre-prepared platform from which to launch their campaign.

German propaganda poster from 1934 reads
'Help Hitler Build – Buy German Products'

Nazi party members listening to a speech by Hitler, 1930

German troops remove the border
barrier between Poland and Germany
during the invasion of Poland, 1939

Germany's first move was to annex an area of
territory in 1938, known a Sudetenland, which
was home to German speaking populations in
Czechoslovakia. Then, in 1939, the Germans prepared
to invade Poland for the purpose of expanding the
German living space. The British warned Germany
that war would be declared if the Germans set foot in
Poland, so Hitler duly instructed his army to encroach
Polish territory on September 1st. Britain declared
war on Germany two days later on September 3rd. As
the Germans moved into Poland from the west, the
Russians invaded Poland from the east as a counter
measure, fearful of Hitler's underlying ambitions.

The Japanese began the second phase of their
invasion of China in 1937 by capturing Beijing. They
then progressively took further swathes of territory.
This was known as the Second Sino-Japanese War,
and Japan did not enter World War II until 1940
when it joined the Axis, having invaded the colony of
French Indo-China, which is now known as Vietnam.

The Political Map

The political map at the beginning of World War II wasn't greatly different from that of World War I, especially in Europe. This was because Germany was again the main protagonist against the Allies, and the countries that joined the Axis either contained Germanic populations or were so dominated by the Third Reich that they had more to gain by siding with the Germans. In the case of Italy, it was led by the Fascist dictator Benito Mussolini, who was an ardent admirer and follower of Adolf Hitler. Thus the European Axis comprised Germany, Italy, Hungary, Romania and Bulgaria. Austria was part of Germany at that time, and known as Anschluss. The Asian wing of the Axis was solely represented by Japan.

To begin with, the European Allies comprised United Kingdom, France and Poland, but many other nations were drawn in on the Allies' side as the war progressed. Asia was represented by Russia and China, while the New World was represented by USA, Canada, Brazil and Mexico. Australia, New Zealand and South Africa were also with the Allies.

As the war moved into 1940 and then into 1941, the political map evolved as the Axis powers invaded new territories. Some conquered nations resisted occupation, while others dealt with their lot by cooperating, for the sake of survival. Similarly, the political map evolved further when the Allies forced the Axis into retreat. A number of European colonies in Asia and Southeast-Asia had become more autonomous under Japanese occupation and resisted having to return to colonial control when they were liberated.

The flags of Fascist Italy and Nazi Germany flying together, 1937

Nuremberg Rally, 1934

Although Russia was on the side of the Allies, it had its own agenda too. While most of the Allies were mainly interested in defeating the Axis and restoring the political map, the Russians saw an opportunity to seize eastern European territories and enlarge their territory, as if Russia wasn't already large enough. The motive behind this was communism. Stalin and his cronies had the vision of a modern world dominated by their particular brand of dictatorial communism, so they wanted the political map to include as much red as possible to counter the blue of democracy and capitalism that they knew would exist following the fall of the Axis.

A few nations were anomalous in their intentions, such as Finland. In effect, it fought its own war, as it battled both the Russians and the Germans. Geographically, Finland was strategically advantageous to invade, providing generous access to the Baltic Sea, but the Finns had no desire to be occupied by either one of the opposed forces.

German troops entering Poland after a 'blitzkrieg'

German soldiers using flamethrowers against a
French bunker on the Maginot Line, 1940

A scene typical of many French towns in northern France with destruction and chaos everywhere following Germany's victory in France in 1940

The Blitzkrieg

Following Germany's invasion of Poland, resulting in the British declaration of war, there was a fallow period of inaction, now known as the Phony War, lasting just over eight months. During this time, Hitler was sizing up the enemy and allowing their forces to become complacent with boredom. He made gestures suggesting that he was hoping they may acquiesce and allow him to keep Poland, but it transpired that he was amassing a large military force ready to invade France and the Lowlands. When the offensive was implemented it caught the Allied forces by surprise. The Germans struck so hard and fast that there was little the opposing forces could do except retreat and attempt to slow down the Nazi advance.

The Germans had introduced a new mode of warfare called Blitzkrieg (Lightning-War). It was designed to be swift and overwhelming, rather like a tsunami, so that resistance was futile. A German officer, named Heinz Guderian had developed the concept in the early 1930s by optimizing tank design along with that of armoured cars and artillery, so that they were highly effective at moving rapidly over rough terrain. He had also fully equipped the tanks and military units with radios, so that communication was state-of-the-art and efficient. As the tanks forged their way forwards, blasting any key opposition units out of action, they were followed by crack divisions of storm troopers, who dealt with the enemy troops while they were still in a state of disarray. To the rear, artillery would be instructed to take out any enemy positions inaccessible to the tanks.

The spearhead of the Blitzkrieg emerged from the Ardennes forest on the 10th May, 1940 and proved unstoppable as it widened and continued westward. Another advantage of its rapid progress was that the Allies were unable to relocate and deploy forces from elsewhere to impede the Blitzkrieg. Added to that, the Allies' equipment was inferior and they had a different strategic mind-set, so they were outgunned and outmanoeuvred. To avoid being killed or being taken captive, the Allies had no choice but to make a rapid tactical retreat and figure out what to do next.

An important factor in the success of the Blitzkrieg was air support. The German air force, the Luftwaffe, was very effective at dive-bombing Allied columns and strategically bombing installations farther afield. This had the effect of weakening supply lines and softening targets to enable the offensive to continue unabated. All in all, the Germans had devised a war machine, which the Allies were unable to counter at that stage of the war, thereby allowing the Germans territorial purchase on mainland Europe.

German soldiers going on the attack
on the Western Front in France, 1940

New Race to the Sea

During the opening stages of World War I, the Allies had been successful in preventing the Germans from reaching the coast of France and Belgium. When it came to World War II, the Allies were not so fortunate. When they realized that the German forces could not be stopped it put a whole new complexion on the situation at hand. The British decided that the best plan of action was to use the sea to their advantage and organize a mass evacuation, thereby leaving the Germans on the coast.

The point of evacuation was to be a small French town named Dunkerque (Dunkirk) and the operation, named Dynamo, began on 27th May, just seventeen days after the Blitzkrieg had begun. On the 28th May, the French army began defending the area around Lille to stall the Germans and give the British a chance to get away. They held up for four days before the Germans punched their way through, but it had done the trick. By the 4th of June the evacuation was complete, so that most of the British force had escaped, along with many French soldiers.

The port Dunkirk shrouded in smoke after fires
had been started by German bombing

Over nine-hundred vessels had been used to evacuate 198,000 British and 140,000 French troops back to British shores. The majority of the rescue fleet had been non-military boats responding to the crisis and risking shellfire to stow as many soldiers as they could. Some craft made several round trips over the nine days of evacuation, which saved a third of a million combatants from death or incarceration. More importantly, it meant that the Allies still had an intact fighting force, albeit stationed on the wrong side of the English Channel, or la Manche as the French call it.

So, the Germans had won the Battle of France in some style, but that was just one battle with many more to come. A little over four years later, many of those evacuees would return to French shores as part of the Normandy Landings and begin the process of pushing the Germans all the way back to Germany.

The evacuation of Dunkerque has taken its place in British folklore, because it was a classic example of people making the best out of a bad situation. The participation of so many civilians also demonstrated cohesion of spirit against the enemy and gave the British something to be positive about at a time when their future was by no means certain.

The ruins of Dunkirk after the fighting had ceased

Tanks Come of Age

The tank was first conceived by the British during World War I, as a means of crossing the battleground under machinegun fire to break the deadlock of trench warfare. By the close of World War I the French had come up with the design that would become the standard format for tanks as we know them today. The Renault FT had a rotating gun turret mounted on an armoured chassis with the engine positioned at the rear and the driver positioned at the fore. This pattern set the standard that saw tanks evolve into efficient fighting machines during the interwar years.

The Germans developed a series of Panzer tank prototypes over the 1930s. They were considered to be better designed than most of the tanks of the Allies, in terms of reliability, manoeuvrability and weaponry, but it was the Blitzkrieg tactics that made them so much more effective in the field of battle, as it enabled the Germans to avoid one-to-one tank confrontations. The Germans were also the first to fully equip their tank corps with radio communications, which made a vast difference in terms of strategy. The Panzer III and Panzer IV were the models used in the early part of World War II. They were relatively small tanks and by the close of the war the Germans had introduced a medium tank in the form of the Panther and a large tank in the form of the Tiger. The Panther was a particularly effective weapon and set the benchmark for all post-war tanks.

A German Panzer IV, 1941

The Russians prompted the Germans to improve their tanks, because they had a model called the T-34, which proved superior to the Panzers on the Eastern Front. Britain had various Cruiser and Infantry tanks, but also used American General and Sherman tanks. Sherman tanks were cheap to mass produce, which is what the USA did best, so there were plenty available even though they lacked sophistication and quality. Two or three Sherman tanks against a Panzer were always going to win,

even though inferior in design. In the end this was a critical factor against the Germans, as they lacked the resources to manufacture enough of their tanks, partly because their quality standards were too high. The Japanese had well designed tanks too, but they were not frequently used due to geography. In fact, they kept many of their tanks in reserve in case they had to defend their homelands, so they were never used. The Chi models of tank were the most advanced of the Japanese designs.

Panzer units of the German Army pass through a blazing Russian village

Turret crew of a 1st Royal Tank Regiment A9
Cruiser Mk I tank at Abbasia, Egypt

A US M4 Sherman tank

Aeroplanes Come of Age

The aeroplane was still in its infancy during the years of World War I, it began life as a reconnaissance vehicle, but its potential as a weapon was becoming evident as more reliable and faster models were being produced. By the close of the war, the aeroplane was beginning to evolve into particular classes of aircraft too, so that the concept of fighters and bombers had emerged.

During the interwar years the aeroplane continued to evolve rapidly. As engines developed to become more powerful relative to size, this meant that faster, stronger and heavier aeroplanes could be engineered.. The aeroplane was no longer a flimsy, slow moving target, but a sleek, fast-moving war machine.

With increased speed, most aeroplanes became monoplanes to optimize their performance and manoeuvrability, and most adopted the standard format of fuselage with two flight wings to the fore and tail-plane to the rear. Other designs were all variations on the same theme even though they could be quite varied in detail.

Henschel HS 123 Dive Bomber, This single-seat biplane with swastika was originally used by the German Luftwaffe during the Spanish Civil War

Japanese seaplane wrecked during the battle of Makin, November 1943

The wreckage of a German Heinkel bomber which crashed on the north-east coast of Britain after an encounter with RAF fighters

German machine gunner in a military aircraft, 1939

Bombers needed to have large wing areas and a number of engines to provide sufficient payload, not just for bombs, but also for the fuel necessary for long-distance missions and the crews need to fly, navigate and defend the aircraft. Fighters needed to be single-engined with relatively low wing area to make them fast and acrobatic in the air. They needed to carry sufficient fuel to escort bombers, but they had only a single pilot and machineguns as additional payload.

There were intermediate aeroplanes too, in the form of fighter-bombers, which were somewhere between the two in terms of size, speed and payload. They were designed for medium range missions, where they could fly alone and make more precise bombing raids at low altitude. The Germans developed a fourth types of combat aeroplane, known as the dive-bomber. The idea was that the aircraft would dive towards its target and jettison its bombs forwards before levelling off. That way, it could hit the target with deadly precision.

A range of support aircraft were also developed for various purposes. There were cargo planes to transport supplies, equipment and personnel. There were also light aircraft for reconnaissance work and for covert field operations. A number of seaplanes were also developed to utilize flat-water for landing and taking off where runways were unavailable. Many fighters were also adapted for use on aircraft carriers, which were basically mobile runways and fuelling depots.

A squadron of German Messerschmitt 110
fighter-bombers flies in formation

The Battle
of Britain

Having conquered France and driven the British
expeditionary force back across the English
Channel, Hitler had designs on invading the
British Isles, which he called Operation Sea Lion. In order
to prepare for the planned invasion he knew that it was
essential to first take on the RAF, so that the British
would lack the air support necessary to defend their
coastline against the offensive. So, the Luftwaffe was
tasked with the job of destroying the British air force.
The ensuing war for air superiority became known as the
Battle of Britain.

As the Battle of Britain was primarily fought in the air, it
meant that fighters were the key aircraft. The British had
the Hurricane and the Spitfire at their disposal, while the
Germans had the Messerschmitt Me109 and the twin-
engined Messerschmitt Me110. In terms of hierarchy,
relating to all-round performance, the Spitfire came
first, followed by the Me109, then the Hurricane and the
Me110. This gave the British the technical advantage,
but they had fewer aircraft, so the odds were about even.
Britain had just short of two thousand aeroplanes, while
Germany had just over two and a half thousand.

Strategy, tactics and intelligence were therefore central
to tipping the odds in favour of the British. Hugh Dowding
had the position of Fighter Command at the start of the
battle, on 10th July, 1940. He implemented very efficient
ways of utilizing the resources available to him. In
particular, he had small squadrons scattered across the
country and an advanced radar system, which allowed
pilots to be scrambled at a moment notice to intercept
enemy aircraft. By a process of attrition, the Luftwaffe
was systematically depleted of its aircraft, until the
battle was declared won by the British on the 31st
October, 1940.

A Spitfire I, one of the first to be supplied to the RAF

Hawker 'Hurricane' planes from no,111 squadron

The British Prime Minister, Winston Churchill, was moved to say "Never before, in the field of human conflict, was so much owed, by so many, to so few." In winning the Battle of Britain, the RAF had caused Hitler to postpone Operation Sea Lion until the following year. By then, his concerns lay at the Eastern Front and Britain was left to lay its plans for an eventual counter offensive. In anticipation of a possible invasion, Churchill had also said "We shall fight on the beaches, we shall fight on the landing grounds, we shall fight in the fields and in the streets, we shall fight in the hills; we shall never surrender," but as it turned out the Battle of Britain had prevented that eventuality.

Operation Barbarossa

Following the German invasion of Poland in 1939, Hitler had agreed a pact of non-aggression with Russia in August of that year. At the time it suited Hitler to pretend that he had no interest in invading Russia, so that he could concentrate his resources in Western Europe. By the close of 1940 Hitler decided that he only needed an occupying force in the west, so he made plans to break his pact with Russia and head eastward. In the spring of 1941 deployed a huge fighting force along the Eastern Front and launched their offensive, named Operation Barbarossa, on June 22nd.

At first, the German assault was a success, as it had been on the Western Front. The Blitzkrieg tactics worked well and the Germans made rapid territorial gains. Hitler was delighted with progress and had every confidence that Moscow would be taken, so that Russia would become
part of the Third Reich. However, things began to go wrong as winter closed in on the Germans. Muddy ground made it difficult for the frontline to move forward and it made the supply chain inefficient. In addition, the troops were ill-equipped to operate in the wet, cold conditions. When the Russian winter set in properly it was so cold that engines wouldn't start and soldiers were suffering from frostbite. The mighty German army had been halted by the Russian climate.

Volunteer American pilots during the Battle of Britain

Russian soldiers in the snow during winter 1941- 1942 on the Russian Front

In addition, the Russian population was so large that Stalin had an almost endless supply of new troops. They died in vast numbers, but were replaced in equally vast numbers, so that attrition was gradually depleting German resources. Being used to their own climate, the Russians were also far better equipped, both physically and mentally, to cope with the conditions.

By December 1941 the Germans were only a matter of miles from Moscow, when Stalin gave the order for the Russian counter-offensive on December 5th. The Germans were unable to defend their positions and were pushed into a momentum of retreat. By mid-December the weather was so cold that the Luftwaffe were unable to assist, because their aeroplanes were rendered inoperative by the sub-zero temperatures. Operation Barbarossa had turned from success to failure as the Germans were pushed ever farther west. Until weather conditions improved in 1942 there was little they could do to try turn matters back in their favour.

The Blitz

About halfway through the Battle of Britain, on September 7th 1940, the Germans began a strategic bombing campaign of British cities. It became known as the Blitz, not to be confused with the Blitzkrieg and would last for over eight months. The initial incentive for the bombing campaign was to strike at factories dedicated to the manufacture of aircraft, munitions and other equipment. Ports were also targeted to disrupt supply lines. However, bombing was not an accurate science in those days, especially under cover of darkness, so the majority of bombs missed their intended targets and randomly hit residential areas, killing many civilians.

Devastated buildings around St Paul's Cathedral, London, after an air raid during the Blitz

Firemen at work on fires, the result of bombs dropped
by the Germans, near St Paul's Cathedral, London

The main cities bombed were London, Birmingham,
Bristol, Plymouth, Birmingham, Southampton and
Portsmouth. London suffered more bombing raids
than the others combined, so sheltering became a
matter of routine. In fact there was an average of
around one raid every three or four days, so it was
better to be safe than sorry. London lost more than
a million homes and over forty thousand people lost
their lives. Things were so dangerous that children
had to be evacuated to live with families in rural
locations for the duration. Despite the death and
carnage visited on their city, Londoners displayed
a behavioural cohesion known as the Blitz spirit,
which saw people helping one another to cope with
the practical problems and the emotional trauma
experienced by so many.

Due to the inaccuracy of bombing, it was a matter
of hit or miss as to whether strategic targets
received bomb damage. Some raids were successful
in halting British progress, but never for sustained
periods of time. They also became self-defeating

as the Blitz only prompted the British to mount
retaliatory raids over Germany, so that their own
wartime industries were disrupted. This tit-for-
tat bombing continued as the war protracted, but
civilian deaths became an ethical issue. For one
thing, the killing of children, women and the elderly
seemed entirely unnecessary. From the British
point of view, there was also the notion that many of
the German civilian population were not followers
of the Nazi ideology, and were therefore innocent
victims. Following the war, those who commanded
and took part in bombing raids were not properly
celebrated and recognized for their contribution to
the war effort. This was because of an undercurrent
of shame that the bombing of civilian areas had
become a component of war. It didn't sit well
with the idea that war should be conducted in an
honourable way.

North Africa Campaign

The North Africa Campaign began when the British decided it would be strategically useful to control the Mediterranean Sea, with a view to launching a counter-offensive against the European Axis from the south. At the time, the region was occupied by Italian forces. The Italians were no match for the British and were pushed into retreat, but Hitler responded by deploying German forces under the command of Erwin Rommel and the complexion of the campaign changed very quickly. There was now parity between the Allied and Axis forces, which resulted in a protracted series of battles, causing the frontline to sweep back and forth as offensives and counter-offensives were launched.

The campaign began in June 1940 and would drag out until May of 1943. The Second Battle of El Alamein (Oct-Nov 1942) is recognized as a seminal moment in World War II, because it was the first time the Allies had achieved a decisive victory against the Axis. Responding to news of the German defeat, Winston Churchill commented in a speech "Now this is not the end. It is not even the beginning of the end. But it is, perhaps, the end of the beginning". He wanted to accentuate the positive outcome, but he also wanted to make it clear that the war was a long way from being won. Following the eventual Allied victory, he commented that the battle had indeed been a turning point in the war as, from that point onwards, the Germans were on the back foot. Momentum had shifted in the Allies' favour.

Below; Two soldiers belonging to the Commonwealth and Allied forces aim at a German soldier surrendering atop his tank 25 October 1942 as a sandstorm clouds the battlefield at El Alamein

British tanks proceeding along the waterfront in
Benghazi as the 8th Army advance in Libya

The first British tank enters Tripoli, Libya with
soldiers and a piper aboard the Valentine tank

Scottish Cameron Highlander
and Indian troops marching past
pyramids, part of Allied defence
preparations against Italian attack

The North Africa Campaign was characterized by the desert terrain, typical of the coastline of the southern Mediterranean. This meant that there was no cover, either from the elements or from enemy fire. Tanks, howitzers and field guns played a central role in the theatre of battle, but the most critical element was one of logistics. As one side advanced, its supply lines became progressively stretched over barren terrain, making it harder and harder to keep the front moving. At the same time, this meant that the supply lines of the opposing force were shortened, making it easier to reach the frontline. As a result, the battle front oscillated west-east/east-west a number of times, until attrition of the German reserves finally allowed the Allies to get the upper hand. The Axis was ultimately forced out of North Africa because sufficient reserves were not made available by Hitler, as he had more pressing concerns elsewhere.

Attack on Pearl Harbor

Late in 1941, the Japanese had plans to invade the southern reaches of Southeast Asia, including the northern coast of Australia. The indefatigable progress of the Nippon army had the Australians deeply fearful and the Americans were amassing a large fleet in the Pacific, in anticipation of their entry into the war. The Japanese were aware of the US military build-up and decided to force the situation in order to prevent the Americans from halting their empire building.

As the Japanese had not yet declared war on the USA they had a trick up their sleeve-the element of surprise. On the morning of December 7th, they launched an all-out offensive against the US military base at Pearl Harbor, Hawaii. The majority of the US fleet was moored-up in the harbour, so it was like shooting fish in a barrel.
The Japanese used over three hundred and fifty aircraft and a number of mini-submarines to wreak havoc on the Americans before they knew what was happening.

The USS California on fire in Pearl Harbor

Many important US vessels were destroyed and sunk during the attack, leaving the American fleet seriously depleted. However, the Japanese had failed to destroy many of the essential dock facilities, which meant that recovery was reasonably rapid. Also, both of the US aircraft carriers and their escort convoys happened to be away from port at the time of the attack, so the core of the US fleet remained intact.

In effect, the Japanese had awakened a sleeping giant by attacking Pearl Harbor in the way they did, without declaring war. While the Japanese celebrated what they saw as a cunning victory, the Allies saw the assault as an underhand ambush. In 1937 the Japanese had behaved in a similar way by opening hostilities against China without declaring

war. In repeating this unsporting approach, the Japanese had done themselves no favors as it revealed an underlying disrespect for other nations and fuelling Allied determination to put them in their place.

Once the USA was committed to the war, it wanted revenge for Pearl Harbor, so the Japanese had determined foe on their tail. It took some time for the Americans to replenish their fleet and develop the right strategy for dealing with ensconced Japanese occupying forces, but eventually they were systematically flushing the enemy from one island after the next and forcing the Japanese to constrict their ambitions of empire.

Troops salvage the wreckage following the attack on Pearl Harbor

Henri Philippe Petain (left), French general
and later Chief of State of Vichy France

American troops wade ashore near Oran, Algeria,
during Operation Torch, November 1942

Vichy France

Following the Fall of France in the Summer of 1940, the French government felt compromised into reached a peace agreement with Germany in order to save France from being portioned out between the Axis powers. In effect, France became a state of the Third Reich, known as Vichy France. The northern region remained occupied by German forces to defend against possible invasion from across the English Channel, while the southern region was the 'free zone' and maintained its sovereignty.

General Charles de Gaulle had fled to exile in London, from where he rallied support against German occupation of France. He also maintained political opposition towards Marshall Philippe Pétain who had assumed leadership of the regime in collusion with the Germans. Many of those still living in France, who opposed Pétain and the Germans, joined the French resistance movement, named the Maquis. Many of the rest of the population did their best to support and assist the Maquis in their terrorist operations, by hiding weapons and protecting people when they could.

There was also a Europe-wide resistance network to help enemies of the Axis travel through occupied Europe without being captured. This included downed airmen, escaped prisoners, special agents, covert operatives, Jews and fellow resistance personnel.

Algeria, in North Africa, was a French colony when Germany conquered France, so it became part of Vichy France, providing the Axis with control of Algeria in 1940. However, the Vichy army offered only half-hearted resistance against the Allies when they decided to invade Algiers in November 1942, because many were reluctantly fighting for the Axis. As a result, Operation Torch was a success and gave the Allies a solid foothold on the southern Mediterranean coast. This contributed to the British success at El Alamein, because it improved supply lines at a critical juncture.

By chance, the commander in chief of the French Navy, Admiral François Darlan, had travelled to Angiers the day before the invasion and was captured. He turned against the Vichy government by deciding to express allegiance with the Allies. As a result Hitler sent reinforcements to North Africa and ordered the occupation of Vichy France by German and Italian troops to protect the Mediterranean coast of France. However, in North Africa the tables were already turning in favor of the Allies, whose next move would be to make preparations for invading Italy.

War in the Atlantic

As World War II progressed, Britain and its allies relied ever more heavily on goods and equipment being shipped from the Americas across the Atlantic Ocean. As a result, the Atlantic became a hunting ground for German submarines, which were known as U-boats. As any large vessels were quite likely to be carrying goods essential for the Allied war effort, in one way or another, the U-boats targeted indiscriminately with their torpedoes. This meant that ships were theoretically safer travelling in convoy, with armed escorts. However, it was double-edged sword, as groups of ships made much easier targets for the U-boats. They were more likely to make a hit and they also had the chance to sink a number of boats in a single raid.

The U-boats also found easy pickings along the American coast. As the Americans were not initially involved directly in the war, they had a rather naïve understanding of the U-boat threat. In particular, they made no effort to blackout their cities, which meant that cargo vessels were nicely silhouetted against the lights at night, making them extremely easy targets for the submarines. They just had to sit in wait and fire torpedoes at will.

German sailors crouch down by the U-boat's conning tower as they manoeuvre against an attack by American B-25 Mitchell and B-24 Liberator bombers, 1944

American aircraft Douglas Dauntless dive-bombers used during great Battle of Midway against Japanese in the Pacific War

Battle of Midway

In June, 1942, the Americans found the Japanese fleet, six months after the Attack on Pearl Harbor, and exacted their revenge. The Japanese had been preparing to attack the Americans at Midway Island, which lies in the North Pacific Ocean roughly halfway between North America and Asia, as its name alludes.

The US force knew the Japanese were somewhere in the area, so they were on the lookout. On the morning of the 4th, a group of US Devastator torpedo bombers located the Japanese and engaged. Most were shot down by the Japanese, but they failed to notice an approaching squadron of thirty-three dauntless dive-bombers dispatched from the USS Enterprise aircraft carrier, and a second squadron of seventeen dauntless dive-bombers from USS Yorktown.

The Japanese defending squadron of Zero fighters had already been scrambled against the Devastators, so they had used their ammunition and were also flying at sea level. When the dive-bombers attacked from above there was nothing the Japanese could do to prevent the US bombs from striking their vessels. Four aircraft carriers were lost to the Americans, along with hundreds of aircraft, and the Japanese no longer had a functioning fleet.

The Japanese had gone to Midway with the intention of finishing off the US fleet but been trounced instead. The Americans got lucky on the 4th June, allowing them to tackle the Japanese fleet virtually untouched, due to fortuitous timing. Thus, the USA had its revenge for Pearl Harbor and turned the war in its favour with one fell-swoop.

The Americans were now able to navigate the warzone with relative impunity, as the Japanese could only dispatch aeroplanes from island bases over a limited flight range. The US then set about systematically taking the islands with airstrips, so that the Japanese were progressively restricted in their military movements and in a perpetual state of defence and retreat. In a maritime theatre of war, having naval supremacy meant victory was inevitable for the US, although it would take another three years of ferocious fighting to achieve, such was the Japanese will.

Group photo of the pilots in an American Navy torpedo bomber squadron prior to the Battle of Midway in which all but one of them would be killed

Smoke from antiaircraft guns fills the sky as aircraft carrier USS Yorktown is hit by a Japanese torpedo during the Battle of Midway

Women at War

World War II marked a significant gender shift in society. Women made a significant contribution to the war effort in a number of direct and indirect ways. Civilian women worked the land and worked in factories to ensure that rations and resources were made available in large enough quantities to satisfy the basic human-needs of the population. Many other women were trained to manufacture munitions, equipment and machines needed in the theatre of battle. They became highly skilled engineers and technicians, and were often better than their male counterparts because they had a finesse and mindset better suited to the exacting work. By taking on these traditionally male roles, they freed up the men to join the forces, where they could be more useful.

That didn't mean though, that women were not enlisted into the forces. There were many supporting roles within the army, navy and air force that women were able to perform. In fact, they had their own equivalent sections within the forces. In the navy they belonged to the Women's Royal Naval Service (WRNS) otherwise known as the 'Wrens'. In the air force they belonged to the Women's Royal Air Force (WRAF) and were known as 'Wrafs'. In the army, they belonged to the Women's Royal Army Corps (WRAC) and were called 'Wracs'. In these sections they performed all kinds of back-up duties, such as operating supply lines, transporting personnel and equipment, repairs, maintenance and administration. Basically, they did any jobs that weren't considered to place them in situations of high risk at the frontline. That didn't mean they were safe however, as many military women fell victim to bombing raids and so on.

Armed service recruiting poster, 1942

Iconic patriotic poster by J. Howard Miller featuring woman factory worker in bandana rolling up her sleeve & flexing her arm muscles

Indian servicewomen in their traditional saris – they are members of the Women's Royal Naval Service, Women's Auxiliary Army Corps, and the Auxiliary Territorial Service

Women also played an important role in the Royal Army Medical Corps (RAMC) which performed essential work tending the sick and injured in warzones. There was even a Royal Army Dental Corps (RADC) which became officially titled in 1946 in recognition of its value during World War II.

In the WRAF there was a unit called the Air Transport Auxiliary (ATA). This was home to a number of female wartime pilots, whose job it was to deliver and collect military aircraft, so that fighter and bomber squadrons had the serviceable aeroplanes they needed to conduct their missions.

A few women were also involved with the entertainment of troops, as comediennes, singers, dancers and members of musical troupes. Some were music hall celebrities, such a Gracie Fields and Vera Lynn, who would perform with forces orchestras, both in Britain and overseas.

The Holocaust

It is fair to say that the Nazis had an obsessive hatred for the Jewish race, which became the focal point of their ideology. Historically anti-Semitism was rooted in the fact that Jews were allowed to lend money for profit, which was a practice frowned upon by other religions. In addition, the Jews had been uprooted from their traditional home, which meant that they had to live itinerant lives, travelling around Europe to make their living. They inadvertently cultivated a stereotypical image, as outsiders with strange ways and questionable ethics, who kept themselves to themselves and found advantage in other people's misfortune.

As it is always easier to blame others when the chips are down, Hitler and his cronies found it convenient to target the Jews as responsible for the German hyper-inflation during the Great Depression. While the German population generally struggled to avoid destitution,

many Jews seemed to be relatively comfortable, because they existed within a sub-culture. It didn't take much imagination for the Nazis to falsely claim that the Jews had a hand in the fiscal demise of Germany, and it took even less imagination for the general population to believe the Nazis. The power of simple suggestion is potent among people who cannot comprehend the complexity of truth.

The Nazis began their persecution of the Jews by ghettoizing them, to keep them all in one place and out of social circulation. They then began shipping them to remote locations and systematically shooting them, but their scale of ambition was such that they could not process sufficient numbers to keep up with the supply of Jews arriving from all over occupied Europe. This prompted the Nazis to devise more efficient ways of killing Jews and disposing of their remains.

A large group of Jews, escorted by soldiers of the SS, are taken to a concentration camp before the crowds at the roadside

Child survivors of Auschwitz show their
tattooed arms, Poland, February 1945

Nazi leader and war criminal Adolf Eichmann (2nd right)
smiling while German officers cut a Jewish prisoner's hair

In early 1942 Auschwitz, one of the most notorious death camps, began the heinous business of gassing and burning Jews en masse. Any Jews considered useful were housed in a concentration camp and put to labour, while those of no value to the war effort were murdered and incinerated next door. A number of similar camps were constructed to cater for Nazi demand in other regions. The Nazis continued with this ethnic cleansing until the Allies encountered the camps as they advanced across Europe towards Germany. Needless to say, the discovery that the Nazis were capable of such inhumanity to man only fuelled the Allied determination to thoroughly stamp them out of history.

Even to this day, what the Nazis did was so shocking and unspeakable that some people find it hard to believe that it happened. Were it not for the evidence and the witnesses it would indeed be difficult to accept that humans are capable of such horrific crimes against their own species. The way the Nazis engineered the Holocaust was by dehumanizing the Jews to make it easier to commit their wrongs. By removing their clothes and possessions, and shaving their heads, the Nazis removed individuality and personality in the Jews, so that they became a uniform population of clones.

The gates of the Nazi concentration camp at Auschwitz, Poland; the sign above them reads 'Arbeit Macht Frei' - 'Work Makes You Free'

Japanese POWs

While the Nazis' treatment of Jews and other undesirables was despicable, they were relatively less cruel to their POWs in general, although torture and execution were commonplace among prisoners who were suspected of spying against the Third Reich.

The Japanese were the ones who treated their POWs with contempt, because they had the overriding view that all other races were inferior to them. Also, the very idea of surrender or being caught by the enemy went against the Japanese ethos, so those who allowed themselves to become POWs were to be regarded as weak and unworthy of respect. The Japanese would nearly always opt for an honourable death, rather than fall prisoner, and this ideal influenced the way they treated those who chose to remain alive by becoming captive.

British soldiers taken prisoner by the Japanese in Singapore, 1942

The Bataan Death March is one of the most notorious examples of the Japanese treatment of POWs. On April 9th 1942 many US and Filipino prisoners were forced to begin an eighty mile march to the prison camp in which they were to be held, following their capture after the Battle of Bataan. The prisoners were beaten and given insufficient medical care, food and rest, so many died from their injuries, exhaustion and disease along the way. Some were murdered when their condition prevented them from continuing with the journey. There were also a number of death marches from Sandakan to Ranau, in Borneo, where similar treatment of prisoners was standard practice by the Japanese.

For those who survived the death marches, there was worse to come at the hands of those who ran the prison camps. Many were cruelly tortured and starved to death or executed by sword or gun for

no particular reason than the amusement of the Japanese guards and officers, who found their duties tedious and viewed the prisoners as sub-human. In addition to their POW camps, the Japanese also had many internment camps for civilian prisoners, who were also kept in appalling conditions and given woeful treatment.

Many of these civilian prisoners were European colonialists who failed to escape the advancing Japanese. By and large, the native populations of invaded territories were allowed to continue their lives in freedom, although under Japanese occupation, so that they contributed to the war effort. Many indigenous peoples enjoyed a new found liberation from servitude when the Japanese arrived, because their colonial bosses had either fled or been incarcerated. This prompted a general shift towards political independence across the region following the war.

Japanese soldiers march prisoners of war, with arms raised, across the Bataan peninsula in what became known as the Bataan Death March, Luzon, Philippines

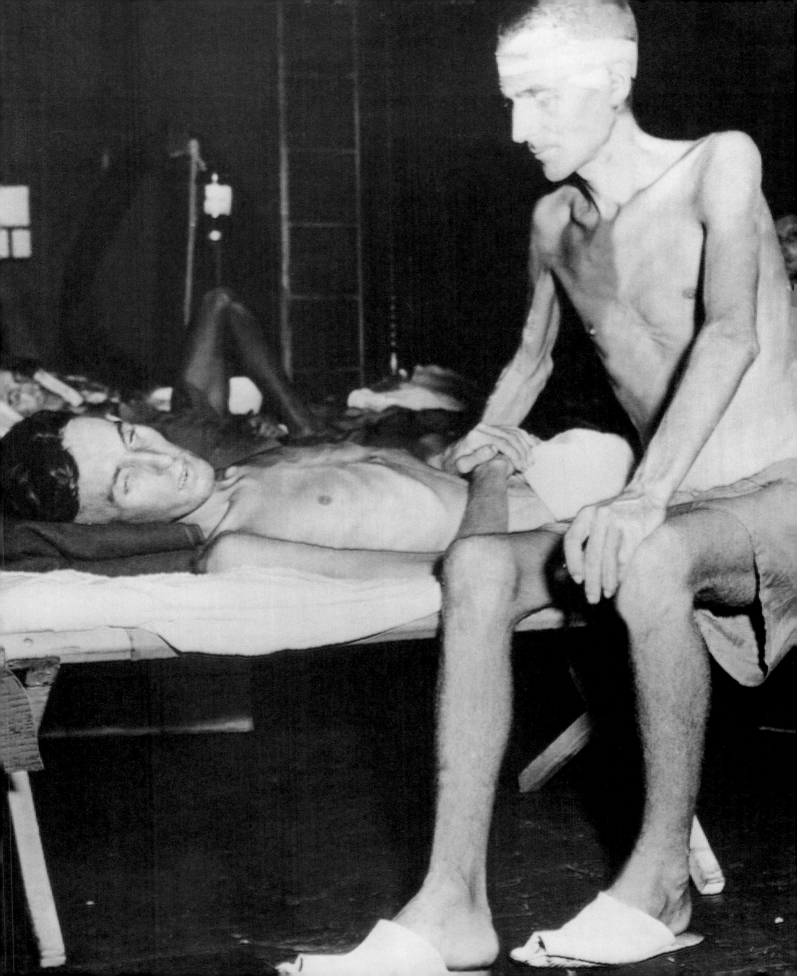

American troops wading ashore from a landing craft
during the World War II Allied invasion of Italy

Italy Campaign

Winston Churchill described Italy as the soft underbelly of Nazi occupied Europe. The Italians were not renowned for their fighting ability, having been easily beaten back by the Allies in North Africa. Hitler was aware that the Mediterranean coast presented a point of vulnerability, but by 1943 he was occupied with developments on the Eastern Front, and he wasn't entirely sure where the Allies might try their luck at a counter offensive. France offered the most practical landing points, so Axis forces had been stationed along the French coast in anticipation of defensive action.

The Allies went for Italy, precisely because it seemed an unlikely strategic choice and was therefore not defended as well as it might have been. On the 10th July, the Allies mounted an assault of the island of Sicily, to give them a foothold on Italian soil, from where they could launch their offensive of mainland Italy. By the time the Allies were ready for the second phase they had, of course, lost any element of surprise and Hitler had deployed German forces to counter the threat, but the Allied occupation of Sicily was key, as it provided a base for naval, army and air forces. This meant that the Allies could attack with sufficient resources to be certain of making successful landings on the Italian coast.

Italian soldiers surrendering after the landing of allied forces in Sicily

The invasion proper began on 3rd September, with British troops landing on the 'toe' of the Italian peninsula. This was called Operation Baytown. Realizing that the Allies meant business, the Italian government surrendered on 8th September, but the Germans intended to fight. The next day, two Allied invasion forces launched assaults in different regions. Operation Slapstick hit Taranto, in the 'arch of the foot' of the Italian Peninsula. The combatants met with little resistance, as the Germans were expecting an invasion attempt of the west coast. Meanwhile, Operation Avalanche struck the beaches of Salerno, on the 'shin' of the Italian peninsula. Here, the Germans put up fierce resistance and it took quite a battle for the Allies to establish a beachhead.

Mussolini's Mistakes

Benito Mussolini rose to power in Italy in 1926, when he seized power as the leader of a fascist regime, in imitation of Adolf Hitler. In 1930 he named himself as Il Duce. Just as Hitler had seduced the Germans with the idea of the Third Reich becoming a new German empire, so Mussolini sold the idea of the 'New Roman Empire' in allusion to the illustrious past of his race.

Things went well for Mussolini until World War II revealed his incompetence as a military tactician, which led the Italian population to turn against him. One major setback was Italy's defeat in North Africa, alongside the Germans, which resulted in the loss of Italian colonial interests. When Operation Barbarossa began on the Eastern Front, Mussolini sent an Italian corps to contribute to the Axis war effort, even though Hitler had not expected the Italians to take part. Mussolini clearly wanted to curry favour with Hitler and have the opportunity to save face by showing that the Italians were a fighting force equal to the Germans. When the tables turned in favour of the Russians, the Italian people were none too impressed by Mussolini's pandering at the expense of many lives.

Then, when the Allies invaded Sicily, on 10th July, it was the final straw. The Italian industrial infrastructure and home front had taken a battering from Allied bombing, so the population had low morale. Mussolini had tried and failed to persuade Hitler to make peace with the Russians, so that Axis forces could be diverted to Italy to prevent an Allied invasion. Most of the Sicilians actually welcomed the arrival of the Allies and the Italian army was on the point of collapse.

On the night of 24/25th of July, Mussolini was arrested by the Italian military police. The Fascist Grand Council had decided to oust him from power and he was imprisoned. When Hitler learnt of Mussolini's arrest he launched plans for Germany to take control of Italy by arresting the entire government and royal family. The plan was to reinstate Mussolini as a puppet leader, in the interests of the Axis. The Italians then concealed Mussolini's whereabouts from the Germans by moving him about.

On September 12th, Mussolini was rescued from captivity by the Germans. He was then forced, by Hitler, to establish a new fascist regime in northern Italy, named the Italian Social Republic. He remained as puppet leader until April 1945, when he was caught by anti-fascist partisans as he made his way to Switzerland in order to escape to Spain by air. On the 28th he was summarily executed. His body was then hung on display in Milan to satisfy the people that he had got what he deserved, especially for the murder of many Italian partisans.

Mussolini arrested in Rome

Aerial view of the German city of Hamburg
which was heavily bombed by the RAF

Razed to the Ground

In the early hours of the 25th July, 1943, the German city of Hamburg received the first of a series of major bombing raids by the RAF. As the bombers neared their target they released a cloud of foil strips to confuse radar systems, so that the Germans saw only a mass of interference on their screens. Then, in the space of an hour the British dropped 23 hundred tons of bombs across the city. Much of Hamburg was razed to the ground by the bombing, but worse was to come for the inhabitants when the ruined city was engulfed by a firestorm.

It began as a number of small fires left burning after the bombing raid had passed. Conditions happened to be dry, warm and breezy, which allowed the fires to begin spreading. As they met up, there was an exponential increase in heat, so that a conflagration developed. Soon, the convection currents generated by the rising heat were so powerful that air was sucked towards the fire from all directions. The wind was strong enough to suck debris and people into the fire and the surrounding area became so hot with radiation that people were roasted some distance away. Thousands of civilians had been hiding in air raid shelters. They survived the initial bombing but fell victim to the firestorm by succumbing to heat, hypoxia and carbon-monoxide poisoning. Twenty-thousand lost their lives and sixty-thousand were hospitalized.

A devastated area of Hamburg, Germany, after a bombing during the Second World War.

The V-1 was a form of unguided missile developed by the Germans in World War II, it was knick named the 'doodlebug', 'or buzz bomb'

Operation Crossbow

astidious aerial reconnaissance by British intelligence had revealed that the Germans were developing secret weapons. In 1943 Operation Crossbow was initiated as a counter measure to these developments. Photographs betrayed the existence of mysterious objects and installations in various locations, in Germany and France. At first British command didn't quite know what to make of interpretations of the photographs, because they were taken from above at altitude. There was uncertainty about what the pictures showed, and there was uncertainty about whether they were real or just decoys designed to fool the Allies into launching wasted bombing raids.

However, images from a site at Peenemünde on the German Baltic coast convinced the Allies that the Germans were indeed working on advanced weaponry. Outlines and shadows suggested flying weapons of one kind or another and indicated that German technology was more advanced than that of the Allies.

The evidence was sufficient to launch Operation Hydra, as part of Crossbow, on the 17th August, which was a strategic bombing raid of the Peenemünde site. The Allies had been correct in their assessment of the evidence, as the site was where the German V-2 Rocket was being prototyped and the V-1 flying bomb was undergoing test flights.

Injured civilians are assisted by rescue workers after a German V-2 rocket exploded in Farringdon Road, London, 1945

After their surrender, a group of German V-2 rocket scientists pose with members of the US 7th Army, 44th Infantry Division, near Oberammergau, Germany, May 2, 1945

The bombing set developments back and caused the scientists and engineers to relocate, but it also made it clear that the Allies were wise to the V-weapons programmes. In the long-term it meant that the Allies could do little to prevent the V-1 and V-2 from being perfected by the Germans and then being mass produced and used in anger against them.

As Operation Crossbow continued into 1944, attention turned to the launch sites for the weapons, which were being constructed all over north-western Europe. The V-1 used a conspicuous launch ramp and the weapons were housed in hockey-stick shaped sheds, making them fairly easy to spot and destroy. The V-2 was more problematic as it had a longer range and required only a portable launch pad, making it undetectable prior to use. However, the Germans had initially intended to store and launch V-2 rockets from a heavily fortified bunker called La Coupole (The Dome), at the northern tip of France.

It was so heavily bombed by the Allies in the Summer of 1944 that the Germans were forced to abandon the site before its completion.

Tunisia Campaign

On 13th May, 1943, Winston Churchill received a message, reading "The Tunis campaign is over. All enemy resistance has ceased. We are masters of the North African shores." The news came two months prior to the Allied invasion of Sicily, where the war was about to be taken from Africa to continental Europe. It marked the beginning of the end for the Axis powers.

Before World War II, Tunisia was a French protectorate, with 250,000 French and Italian colonists. It became the last remaining enclave for the Axis powers after a series of North African battles and the Allied campaign to finally defeat the enemy outright began on 17th November 1942.

Initially the combined German and Italian force did well, but the Allies had the logistical advantage. They had open supply lines to keep equipment,

provisions and personnel pouring into the theatre of battle, so it was just a matter of time before the Axis force was cornered in the city of Tunis and faced with annihilation or surrender - they chose the latter.

Some military historians regard the Tunisia Campaign as one of the tactical errors that led to the demise of the Nazi regime. Hitler's motive for sending in so many German troops was to keep the Mediterranean under Axis control, so that an Allied invasion remained impracticable. In reality it only delayed the inevitable by six or so, and it cost Hitler dearly in terms of available manpower and resources. He would have been better off by evacuating North Africa and consolidating his defenses on the European Mediterranean coast.

American M4 Sherman tank racing along during the desert fighting between US and German forces in the El Guettar Valley

German troops after the capture of Tebourba, Tunisia, 1942

In hindsight, it is possible that he may have successfully beaten the Allies back from Italy in September 1943, but that is a matter of pure conjecture. After all, he was also in the process of stretching the Axis too far on the Eastern Front. Fundamentally, Hitler's ambitions of conquest got the better of his common sense, because he wasn't guided or motivated by military strategic thinking. He wanted too much too soon, so that he could live up to the promise he had made to the German people, and in his haste to demonstrate his omnipotence he made basic errors of judgement, so blinded by his ego that he could not listen to the advice offered by his military commanders.

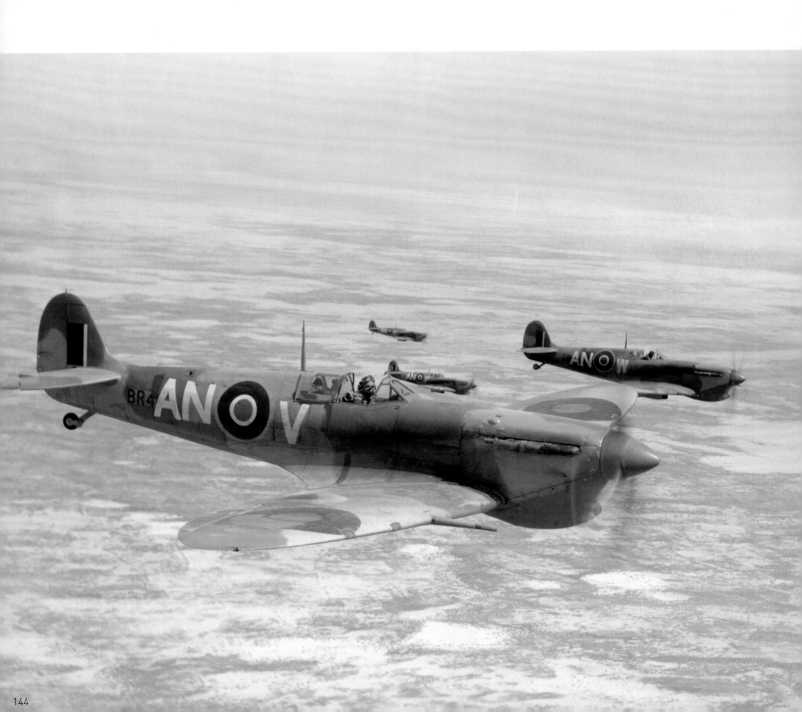

Royal Air Force flying in loose formation
over the Tunisian desert providing cover
for Allied bombers, April 1943

A B25 bomber taking off from the USS
Hornet on a bombing raid of Tokyo

Pacific Sweep

Following the Battle of Midway, in 1942, the
Japanese were limited in their ability to
defend their interests, making it easier for the
Allies to begin the process of pushing the invaders
back towards their own archipelago. Nevertheless, it
wasn't going to be an easy process, because Japan's
territorial gains comprised a great many islands of
different sizes, so that each required its own battle
on one scale or another. Also, the Allies would need
to mount assaults from sea to land, making them
extremely vulnerable to defensive fire while the
Japanese were concealed in networks of tunnels,
trenches and bunkers on higher ground.

When the Americans began their sweep of the
Pacific islands they knew that the holed-up Japanese
garrisons were isolated by the retreat of the Japanese
force as a whole. This meant, it was a matter of
attrition in order to take each island. The Americans
began by bombarding an island with shells fired from
warships placed some distance away, and bombs
dropped by aircraft, whilst the landing party prepared
to make their assault and establish a beachhead.

Japanese kamikaze putting on his forehead
bandeau with rising sun, 1944

Despite efforts to destroy enemy positions, the Japanese would often survive in significant numbers and have sufficient weaponry to put up fierce resistance. So, the Americans had to adopt a systematic approach to flushing the Japanese from their lairs. This involved the use of flamethrowers and grenades to either kill or force the Japanese into the open. They were usually shot as they emerged, because they were inclined to have one last attempt at aggression in order to die honourably. Very few surrendered themselves to the Americans, as that was considered such a shameful way to behave.

On the larger islands of Southeast Asia, the situation was rather different, because the theatre of battle was tropical jungle, which presented a different set of problems. In particular, there was the lack of visibility in the thick vegetation. This meant that platoons of Allied and Japanese troops would fall upon one another by chance and enter into battle at close quarters, often involving hand-to-hand combat. In both types of situation, casualty numbers were high, but the Allies gradually and methodically swept the Japanese back to whence they had come. As the circumference of the Japanese held territory reduced however, then the easier it became for them to defend it, so the fighting became progressively more fierce the farther it moved towards the Japanese archipelago.

View of the USS North Carolina
battleship en route in the Pacific Ocean

The Russians had built an impenetrable barrier. They also had 2.5 million troops, while the Germans had less than 1 million. The also had almost 8,000 tanks, to the Germans' 3,000. They also had 2,800 aircraft, while the Germans had 2,100. And they had 25,000 guns and mortars against the Germans' 10,000. Needless to say, the odds were stacked heavily against the Germans from the off.

The Russians allowed the Germans to exhaust themselves with the futility of attempting to breach the fortified line and then launched counter-offensives. In terms of losses, the Germans faired far better than the Russians, because they were a far better fighting force, but the battle was a decisive victory for the Russians simply because combative attrition had crippled the German force, which was forced into retreat. Sheer strength in numbers had given the Russians the upper hand,

and that is how things remained for the rest of the war.

By the springtime of 1944, the Russians had retaken the Ukraine and were well on their way to pushing the Germans back across Eastern Europe. The Third Reich was steadily constricting from the east and from the south. Soon it would be constricting from the West too, as the Allies were planning a mass invasion of German occupied France, so that Hitler's empire could be dissolved and eroded from all sides. The Russian army was particularly shocked by discovering the way the Nazis had treated the Russians under their occupation and this resentment grew as they closed in on the regime. Prospects were very grim for any Nazis who were caught by the Russians.

Germans in the Ukraine making their
escape from the approaching Russians

A German soldier sitting with his head in
his hands by a destroyed heavy artillery
gun following the Battle of Kursk

Plans for Invasion

In order to achieve a successful invasion of Nazi-occupied France it was necessary for the Allies to organize Operation Overlord in as much secrecy as possible. However, it was impossible to conceal the vast build-up of troops and military equipment necessary for the offensive. This meant that the only real secrets were the time and location of the invasion, so the Allies played this to their advantage.

As the shortest route across the English Channel was between Dover and Calais, the Allies decided to work on the idea that Hitler could be persuaded that this was the intention if they used every trick in the book to deceive Hitler.

Decoy tanks and aircraft were positioned near to the Dover coast to fool German reconnaissance into believing that invasion preparations were under way. Some decoys were fabricated from wood and canvas, others were inflatable rubber, but they appeared very convincing from a bird's eye view. False radio messages were also transmitted, so that German intelligence sent erroneous information to Hitler.

Meanwhile, efforts were made to conceal the genuine invasion preparation activity going on at or near a number of ports farther to the west on the English south coast. The troops themselves were kept in the dark about the details of the invasion. They were housed at barracks inland, so that they had no idea where they would embark on the fateful day.

American Sherman tanks and troops move through the damaged and
bombed town of Flere as they move inland from the Normandy beach

The timing of the invasion was not fixed, due to the
requirement for clement weather conditions. This
meant that everything needed to be able to be held
on standby and ready to put into operation at short-
notice, as and when high command pressed the
green light.

Despite the odds against keeping the plans covert,
Hitler remained uncertain about the Allies' plans
and decided to keep the majority of his defensive
force in the Calais area. When the invasion came in
Normandy there was still fierce resistance from the
Germans, but nowhere near as much as there would
have been had Hitler second-guessed the Allies' plans.

In addition, Erwin Rommel happened to be away on
leave, so that German defenses were not commanded
efficiently. Several Panzer divisions could have been
deployed with devastating effect, but Hitler had
refused to move them far enough west and Rommel
was about to persuade him to do so. As it was, the
tanks were too far east, and Rommel was not on the
scene quickly enough to orchestrate any measures to
prevent the Allies from securing a firm foothold.

D-Day

The first day of Operation Overlord came on 6th June, 1944. It was called D-Day, or Zero-Day, so that each subsequent day had a number: D plus 1, D plus 2, and so on. The idea was that certain objectives were met in rapid succession following the landings, to make sure that Germans were unable to mount a counter offensive and keep the momentum on the side of the Allies.

The landing troops embarked on their journey across the English Channel during the night of the 5-6th June. There had been a storm on the 5th and further storms were forecast, so high command had opted to go for a short window in the weather, rather than wait any longer and risk the Germans finding out.

The beaches of Normandy had been given five code names; Utah, Omaha, Gold, Juno, and Sword, running west to east. The fleet assembled mid-channel, having sailed from various locations in southern England and Wales, and then headed for their fate with destiny. A number of airborne Paratroop units had gone ahead to attack German defensive positions and take bridges near the town of Caen, to prevent the enemy from deploying reserve forces farther west.

US troops march up beachhead while landing craft in rear continue to unload supplies, equipment and men following victorious D-Day invasion

American soldiers aboard an LCI landing craft on its way across the English Channel towards the beaches of Normandy for Operation Overlord

When the landing parties begin their assaults, they were met with varying difficulties, due to the different geography and defensive installations. Omaha beach, for example, was backed by steep cliffs, with machine gun positions at a vantage point. Troops had to rush to the foot of the cliffs and wait until the defences had been destroyed. Utah beach, as it was farthest west, was only poorly defended. The troops had relatively little trouble in establishing a safe beachhead. Elsewhere, resistance was fierce, but the Germans were unable to prevent the Allies from coming ashore and defeating them.

Utah and Omaha beaches were assigned to the US First Army. Sword and Gold beaches were assigned to the British Second Army, and Juno beach was assigned to the Canadian Second Infantry Division. By the evening of the 6th, all five beach zones were safely in Allied hands and the armies had met up with the airborne divisions inland. The next phase of the attack was to consolidate the Allies' position by taking Cherbourg, to the west, and Caen, to the east, before beginning the invasion proper and forcing German lines back towards central Europe.

Meanwhile, there was the matter of supply lines. As the Normandy beaches offered no ports for transport ships to moor up, the Allies used prefabricated floating harbors called 'Mulberries'. They comprised floating section that ran out into deep water, so that vehicles could disembark by driving along a gangway and then use ramps to come ashore. In this way, the Allies managed to off-load all of the military hardware and reserve troops they required in a short space of time, to keep the frontline constantly moving.

The French heroes of D-Day in Quistreham, France on June 06, 1944

The Push

O n D-Day the Allied force numbered 156,000, while the Germans had just 10,000. By the end of the day, 12,000 Allies had lost their lives against the German defensive positions, but the prime objective of Operation Overlord had been achieved. The Germans lost between and half and two-thirds of their men, while the rest were either taken prisoner or managed to retreat.

The subsequent fight to begin pushing the Germans eastward was not going to be easy. Allied high command had been hopeful of bringing the war to an end before the close of 1944, but the Germans had other ideas. The ceasefire of World War I had seen the Allies and Germans leave the field of battle in France and Belgium. This time, the Germans knew they would be chased all the way back to Berlin, so they put up an incredibly fierce resistance all of the way across Western Europe. Also, as the perimeter of the Third Reich gradually shrank, the German forces had less frontline to defend, so their resistance was undiminishing. As a result, many battles ensued as the Germans made tactical retreats to natural obstacles, such as rivers, where they stood their ground.

German soldiers captured during the Battle of Normandy

Despite their best efforts to keep the Allies from advancing, they inevitably failed because of the same logistical imbalance that had been their undoing on the Eastern Front. The Allies had an inexhaustible supply of equipment and reserve troops, while the Germans had finite and diminishing resources. Of course, the German high command knew very well that the situation was hopeless and wanted to sue for peace before the Allies invaded Germany, but Hitler flatly refused to consider surrender as an option. In fact, it seems that he grew so obsessed with the idea that Germany was 'meant' to win the war, that he wouldn't listen to his military officers. So, the war at the Western Front continued despite the eventual outcome being quite obvious.

In Italy, the Allies had reached the Gothic Line, well above Rome and on the Eastern Front, the Russians had entered Poland. It was only a matter of time before Hitler's domain was reduced in size to a smaller area than he had started with. In Asia the Japanese were being pushed out of China and Burma, and in Southeast Asia they were being steadily purged from the many islands. The wars in both the West and in the East were both going well for the Allies and badly for the Axis.

Soldiers of the 5th Allied Army pass a dead German soldier as they push their way through the enemy's mountainous Gothic line of defence in Italy

V-Weapons

Following the Normandy landings on the 6th June 1944, part of the German's defensive strategy was to unleash their secret weapons, the V-1 flying bomb and the V-2 rocket bomb, in an attempt to make the Allies think twice about advancing.

The first V-1 was launched on the 13th June, just a week after D-Day. Between June and October over 9.5 thousand V-1s were fired at London and other parts of Southeast England. Eventually the launch sites were overrun by the Allies as they advanced eastward, so the Germans were only able to continue firing them at targets in Belgium, because the V-1 had a limited range. 12,000 V-1s were successfully launched, but they killed a relatively low number of civilians, at just short of 23,000. With fewer than two casualties per bomb, they had no persuasive effect on the Allies, but they did have a psychological impact. This was partly because the V-1 was propelled by a noisy pulse-jet engine, which would cut-out to allow the bomb to fall. The abrupt end to the noise struck fear into people, because the exact point of contact with the ground was random, so it was matter of waiting for the sound of the explosion.

A V-1 rocket or flying bomb, in flight over the city of London, 1943

The V-2 rocket bomb was a different matter altogether. It flew at supersonic speed, so no one heard or saw it coming. There would be a sudden and unexpected explosion as the ballistic missile struck the ground from a high trajectory. The first of over 3 thousand V-2s was launched on 8th September. They killed an average of about three people, because there was no prior warning of a strike and they carried larger warheads.

The V-1 was essentially an unmanned, or drone, aeroplane. As it was visible, noisy and slow-flying at low altitude, it was fairly easy to shoot down with antiaircraft guns or to intercept with fighter aircraft. The V-2, on the other hand, was state of the art technology and the Allies had no way to counter the threat, apart from preventing it from being launched in the first place. Although the V-2 was a remarkable machine for its time, it was enormously expensive to manufacture. Each V-2 cost the same as a fighter plane, and each V-1 about half that, so Hitler would have been far wiser to have invested in 9 thousand aircraft, which would have been far more effective in defending the Western Front.

Canadian soldiers sitting on a German V-1 bomb which failed to reach its target in Britain

The aftermath of a V1 'doodlebug' flying bomb attack, England, 1944

The Plot Against Hitler

German General Erwin von Witzleben, who was involved in the July Plot to assassinate Hitler – he was tried, found guilty of treason and hanged in 1944

I n July, 1944, only the Nazi party faithful still believed that Hitler could win the war. With the Allies back in France and advancing steadily east, most of the German high command knew the game was up. So, they hatched a plot to assassinate the Fuhrer and then negotiate a peace treaty. A number of partisan assassination attempts had failed over the years, as Hitler was careful to make his behaviour varied and unpredictable, but this time it seemed that the plot could not fail.

On the 20th July, a conspirator named Claus von Stauffenberg attended one of Hitler's military conferences, carrying a bomb concealed in a suitcase. Having planted the bomb beneath the table where Hitler would be standing, Stauffenberg was summoned away to a planned telephone call before the blast was detonated. The explosion wrecked the conference room, but Hitler had survived because the wide leg of the table had shielded him from the blast. He was injured, but not mortally, and immediately set about rounding up the conspirators for execution. Meanwhile, the conspirators had been so confident that Hitler must have died in the explosion, that they revealed themselves by prematurely implementing the next stage of their plan. In so doing, they signed their own death warrants, and Hitler had a much better idea of whom he could trust.

Erwin Rommel, who was blackmailed
by Hitler into taking his own life

Erwin Rommel had agreed to lend his support to the conspiracy against Hitler, which was already afoot in the springtime of 1944. At the time of the bombing Rommel was recovering from battle injuries, but he was clearly implicated. As Rommel was the most popular officer in the German army, Hitler had a problem to solve. If he had Rommel executed and declared a traitor, then it would cause low morale at the Western Front or even initiate mutiny amongst the army with the knowledge that Rommel had lost faith in Hitler. To avoid a possible coup, Hitler decided to inform Rommel that his family and friends would be murdered unless he committed suicide. So Rommel took a cyanide pill on October 14th 1944. The official version of events was that Rommel had either suffered a heart attack or a brain haemorrhage due to the head injuries he had sustained in July.

Allies at the Gates

On the 29th April, 1945, the German army in Italy surrendered to the Allies. Since the autumn of 1944, the Allied and Axis forces had been in a stalemate, but on the 8th April, 1945, the German frontline began to give way. The Germans made a number of tactical retreats but decided to throw in the towel just three weeks later. This was the start of the closing chapter for the Third Reich.

Only three days prior to the German surrender on the Italian front, the Russians had surrounded Berlin and begun their assault on the German capital, where Hitler and his cronies were holed up. On the 20th April, Hitler had celebrated his 56th birthday, undoubtedly aware that it would be his last. Nevertheless, he resolutely kept on barking orders to the army units defending Berlin, determined that Germany would sink in a ball of flames rather than surrender.

A German soldier sits amongst the ruins of the Reichstag in Berlin after the Russian army entered the city in 1945

People crowd on top of a van during VE Day celebrations, London, 8th May 1945

As the Battle of Berlin progressed, the tactics were adapted to street warfare, where every building had to be purged of Nazi resistance. As a result, many civilians died in the crossfire, also, the Russians were in no mood to distinguish between the two, as a German was a Nazi was a German in their view. They had seen evidence of the Nazis inhumanity to man on countless occasions as the Eastern Front had moved west, and sympathy was not an emotion forthcoming. Many Berlin women were raped by the Russians as a gesture of humiliation and revenge.

When the Nazis realized what they could expect at the hands of the Russians, many travelled west to surrender to the Americans and British, knowing they would have a better chance of survival.

Herman Goering, who had fled to Bavaria, telegrammed Hitler to suggest that he took over the leadership, since the Fuhrer was indisposed and unlikely to escape the Russian encirclement. Hitler was furious but powerless to retaliate. On the 28th April he was informed that his army had only two days' worth of ammunition left, so Hitler resigned himself to his fate. He married his mistress Eva Braun on the 29th and both committed suicide on the 30th. Admiral Karl Dönitz succeeded Hitler until Germany officially surrendered to the Allies on 23 May 1945.

VE (Victory in Europe) day was celebrated on 7-8th of May, as that was when hostilities ceased and Allied nations realized that peace had finally arrived after nearly six years of war. However, hostilities had not yet ceased in Asia, where the Japanese were still putting up a spirited and fanatical resistance.

Iwo Jima and Okinawa

As the Americans fought their way nearer to the Japanese archipelago, the enemy battled ever more ferociously. Surrender was not an option for the Japanese mindset, as it was better to die honourably at arms or to commit suicide to avoid the shame of being held prisoner. There was also the incentive of protecting their homeland and the Japanese civilian population. The Japanese army judged the Allies by their own standards and presumed that their people would be harshly treated if they were defeated, so they had every reason to fear their enemy and to fight maniacally to the end. The battles of Iwo Jima and Okinawa have gone down in the annals of history as two of the bloodiest campaigns ever fought.

The Battle of Iwo Jima lasted from February 19th to March 26th 1945. The Allies wanted to take Iwo Jima as a staging post to mount airborne attacks on the Japanese main islands. The prospect of the Americans getting that close to Japan gave the Japanese a resolve that made them very hard to fight. The Japanese force numbered nearly 22,000 and all died bar just 216 who were taken prisoner. More than 99% of the Japanese troops were killed by the Americans before Iwo Jima was secured. This statistic would be very telling in decisions to come about how to win the war.

Soldiers raising the United States flag
at Iwo Jima, February 23, 1945

American soldier under fire of Japanese machine guns in the Death Valley where 125 US soldiers were killed in May 1945 in Okinawa, Japan

It was a similar story with the Battle of Okinawa, fought between April 1st and June 22nd 1945. The Japanese also made use of a kamikaze flying bomb, called the Ohka, which was much like the German V-1, except that it was piloted by a human volunteer, so that it could be aimed precisely at targets, which were usually American ships. The idea of making a certain sacrificing of one's life for the sake of the war effort was alien and disturbing to the Allies, as is indicated a level of fanaticism in the Japanese, suggesting that they would stop at nothing. They also had a kamikaze submarine, called the kaiten, and began using standard aircraft for suicidal bombing missions.

By the time Iwo Jima and Okinawa were in US hands it was clear that a great many more Americans and Japanese would die if it were necessary to take the war to Japan itself. As the Japanese were not about to surrender or to agree to a ceasefire, the Allies had no choice but to continue their advance until a conclusion was met.

An American serviceman shares his rations with two Japanese children in Okinawa, Japan, 1945

Atomic Bomb

Behind the scenes during World War II, the Allies had grown increasingly concerned that the Nazis and the Japanese might be developing nuclear weapons, for it was known that they were experimenting with nuclear technologies. As it happened their scientists had abandoned ideas of atomic weapons before Germany surrendered, but the US had initiated a nuclear weapons program in New Mexico, named the Manhattan Project.

On July 16th 1945, the US scientists conducted their first atomic bomb test, called the Trinity Test. It was an unqualified success and it immediately became apparent that the Americans had a terrifying new weapon that might be deployed against the Japanese to end the remaining war in the Far East.

The decision to go ahead and use the atomic bomb against Japan was not made lightly and was based on a balance of statistics. It was calculated that a continuation of conventional warfare would kill a quarter of a million Americans and several million Japanese. Although the atomic bomb might kill hundreds of thousands, it was hoped that it would force the Japanese to capitulate, so that overall losses were far fewer.

The first of two atomic bombs was dropped on the city of Hiroshima on August 6th 1945, and was named 'Little Boy'. On detonation, two pieces of uranium were fired together to create a critical mass, leading to nuclear chain reaction and a single explosion with sufficient force to annihilate the entire city.

American bomber pilot Paul W. Tibbets Jr. (centre) stands with the ground crew of the bomber 'Enola Gay', which Tibbets flew in the atomic bombing of Hiroshima

A dense column of smoke rises more than 60,000 feet into the air over the Japanese industrial port of Nagasaki, the result of an atomic bomb

The second atomic bomb was dropped on the city of Nagasaki on August 9th 1945 and was named 'Fat Man'. This bomb worked on a different principle, which was also used for the Trinity Test. A sphere of plutonium was surrounded by a shell of conventional explosive, so that detonation caused the plutonium to increase in density and initiate a nuclear chain reaction.

There had been two designs just in case one hadn't worked on the day. In fact, both worked with such devastating effect that the Japanese announced their intention to surrender just five days later. VJ (Victory over Japan) Day was celebrated 14-15th August and the surrender was signed on September 2nd.

It has been estimated that the Hiroshima and Nagasaki bombs killed around a quarter of a million civilians, either in the initial blasts of from injuries and the effects of radiation. It remains a matter of conjecture as to whether that figure would have been exceeded by a conventional conclusion to the war, but it seems likely that it would when considering the Japanese determination to fight or die. Certainly fewer American lives were lost and Japan suffered relatively little collateral damage too.

US servicemen celebrate their return home in Times Square following the long awaited-victory over Japan

The ruins after the atomic bomb attack on Hiroshima

The Shape of Things to Come

During World War II, the Nazi regime made a systematic attempt to eradicate the Jewish race from Europe. Approximately 6 million Jews died in the Holocaust. When the Allies liberated the death camps there was universal condemnation of what the Nazis had done. Not least because it became apparent what humans were capable of doing to other humans in the name of ideology and belief. People preferred to think that the savage side of humanity had been left behind in our prehistory. The Nazis showed that it was still there, lying dormant and ready to rear its ugly head when humans were susceptible to the power of suggestion and persuasion.

This collective enlightenment about the true nature of the human condition seemed to generate a reaction against it, in an effort to ensure that the circumstances for its germination never arose again. From this storm of shock and disappointment in humanity came the idea for a Jewish nation, as compensation for their treatment and a way of salving the conscience of the Allies, as much as the defeated Germans, who recognized that anti-Semitism was really the fault of all.

So, in 1947 the United Nations General Assembly approved the idea of giving the Jews their own homeland, and in 1948 the State of Israel was formed. Unfortunately, it required the partitioning of Palestine, which displaced another population who had lived there for countless generations. Thus, the Israeli Jews have still never known peace and security, because acquiring the land has led to a whole new set of problems.

Goering on trial for war crimes in 1946

As for the Germans, they had to take a long hard look at themselves after the war. Many civilians had either participated in the persecution to some extent, or turned a blind eye to what was going on. There was a general sense of shame that the Nazis had been allowed to take things so far, which led to the unfortunate phenomenon of Holocaust denial. It was easier to deny the truth, despite the overwhelming evidence, by claiming that the evidence was all part of an elaborate conspiracy to discredit the Nazis. That, in itself, provides some idea of just how horrific and unspeakable the Nazi crimes against humanity were.

Following the Nuremburg trials, after the war, many Nazi leaders were executed for their decisions and behavior, which had little or nothing to do with the concept of legitimate warfare, as described by the Geneva Convention. Nazi hunters, bent on revenge and justice, spent decades in pursuit of those Nazis who had managed to escape abroad.

Communist-Socialist
Bloc meeting, 1947

An Independent World

For different reasons, many European colonies, in Asia and Southeast Asia, began a drive for independence following World War II. For some, it was the feeling that they had sacrificed personnel only because they had been ordered to by the colonial powers and had gained nothing in return. For others, it was because falling under Axis control had not been such a bad experience, as they had been given their autonomy for a few years. As a result the world map began to change considerably in the post-war era.

In marked contrast, other countries lost their autonomy, because they were absorbed into the newly formed Soviet Union. Although the Russians had been among the Allies during the war, this was only a nominal status in real terms. The truth was that the Russians were the enemies of Germany, just as the Britain, France and the USA were, but that is where the alliance stopped. Having been the first to Berlin, the Russians wanted a decent sized chunk of Europe as their reward.

It was difficult to argue against, since the Russians had lost about twenty million people on the Eastern Front, so Stalin got what he wanted. East Germany, Poland, Czechoslovakia, Hungary, Romania and Bulgaria all became satellite states of the Soviet Union, as the Communist Bloc.

Stalin's communist regime then became very internalized and secretive, so that the USA and other Western nations became the Soviet Union's enemies in all but name. This state of affairs heightened with the more advanced development of nuclear weapons in the 1950s, so that the Cold War began. In essence, it was a diplomatic stalemate based on the premise of Mutually Assured Destruction (MAD) should a nuclear war ever breakout.

This situation perpetuated until 1991, when the Soviet Union collapsed. The countries of the Communist Bloc had their autonomy restored, as did a fourteen other nations that had been under Soviet control since 1922. Russia remains the largest country in the world.

India, the single biggest British colony, was granted its independence in 1947. It coincided with the partitioning of the region according to religious differences, primarily Hindu and Muslim so that modern India and Pakistan were created. As the Hindus and Muslims were not neatly divided geographically prior to the partitioning, it resulted in a great deal of ethnic bloodshed as people were forcibly displaced and relocated by the process.

Index

Picture Credits

All images featured in this book are courtesy of Getty Images © Getty Images.

Page 168 - Alfred Eisenstaedt/Pix Inc./Time & Life Pictures/Getty Images